Lacey Haynes and Flynn Talbot are sex and relationship coaches, and hosts of the top-charting podcast, Lacey & Flynn Have Sex, in which they have sex live to show the unfiltered reality of sex in long-term relationships. The show has been heard in 180 countries, had over 500k downloads worldwide and been featured in the *Guardian*, the *Sun*, the *Daily Mail* and on ITV's *This Morning*, among others.

Lacey and Flynn live in the countryside with their two young children.

LACEY HAYNES & FLYNN TALBOT

Come Together

The secret to deep, meaningful, elevated sex

PIATKUS

PIATKUS

First published in Great Britain in 2023 by Piatkus

1 3 5 7 9 10 8 6 4 2

A CIP catalogue record for this book
is available from the British Library.

ISBN 978-0-349-43452-0

Typeset in Sabon by M Rules
Printed and bound in Great Britain by Clays Ltd, Elcograf S.p.A

Papers used by Piatkus are from well-managed forests
and other responsible sources.

Piatkus
An imprint of
Little, Brown Book Group
Carmelite House
50 Victoria Embankment
London EC4Y 0DZ

An Hachette UK Company
www.hachette.co.uk

www.littlebrown.co.uk

Note: the names of all those who have shared their experiences have been
changed to protect their privacy.

To Fox for the teachings,
and Rocky for the vision.

Contents

Introduction

It was raining again in the Cotswolds. It was 2019 and the kind of August weather that can't do anything but disappoint in having the audacity to show up on a late summer's day. It was cold. We were wearing rain suits, Lacey also layered in a vintage faux-fur pink winter coat with mother-of-pearl buttons. We took turns carrying our then-two-year-old daughter in a carrier on our backs, Flynn loosening the straps every time to fit them around his six-foot-seven frame, wrapped in layers of waterproofs.

Lacey was teaching at a wellness festival over the weekend. We were staying in a bell tent that had been organised by the festival, as we'd just returned from a three-month stint in Australia to visit Flynn's parents. We didn't know it as we traipsed through the rain, going back and forth between our tent and the teaching spaces, but our lives were about to radically change.

Flynn was deep in a process of disentangling himself from his career and the identity born of his work spanning the previous twenty years. He'd recently hit pinnacle career highlights, representing Australia at Somerset House in London and exhibiting at the Victoria and Albert Museum with large-scale lighting installations. He was cementing himself in the light art and design scene the world over – and yet, something wasn't aligning for him in terms of satisfaction.

He was in that liminal space with which the masculine often contends at some point, reckoning with the achievement of long-held dreams alongside a deeper search for meaning and contentment in day-to-day life. It was a journey that had brought him to this very moment, at an English festival, eating deluxe veggie burgers that were probably giving everyone indigestion, trying to wrangle a toddler and navigating less-than-ideal weather conditions.

The day before, we'd sat on the floor in our tent with our daughter asleep for her afternoon nap in one of the two inflatable beds that turn standard camping into 'glamping'. We'd switched on the fairy lights, made some tea and tried to dry ourselves as we took a moment of respite from the festival noise. Lacey was feeling queasy, probably due to the veggie burgers, but maybe there was another reason. Flynn invited her to lie on the ground. He was offering one of his 'treatments': what he called 'reiki', while smiling because he'd never had reiki done to him, let alone trained in reiki; it was his take on what reiki might be if he'd known anything formal about it. Nevertheless, it always worked.

He made a nest of cotton blankets and sleeping bags and she lay down, pieces of hair sticking to her face with the damp. He breathed deeply and guided her to do the same. There was something both silly and deeply moving about this moment where Flynn offered something about which he knew nothing beyond his own experience. He wasn't trained, and yet he was confident enough to be guided by what he felt. In that moment, he felt drawn down to Lacey's belly, where he hovered his hands.

With the sound of the rain pattering on the canvas of the tent, Flynn fell into a deep meditation. His hands hovered over Lacey's womb-space, connecting to their unborn child, who hadn't been confirmed through a pregnancy test, but whom they'd both felt present. Lacey loved the tenderness of these moments: this powerhouse Australian man who spent most of his time in the logical realm of 3D computer renders, calculations and design challenges, expressing such an aptitude for the tuned-in, spiritual side of life.

His hands moved, exploring the space between his palms and her body, the energetic expanse between two people who know one another deeply and still have much to discover. Lacey fell into a deep sleep, and when she awoke, Flynn sat there wide-eyed.

'I saw a granite mountain rise from your womb,' he said. 'Our son's name is Rocky, like the mountains.'

Lacey actually cheered. We both laughed, and then shushed ourselves, trying to keep from waking our daughter. The queasiness had subsided. We both fizzed with delight – as much as two soggy people can.

Lacey had a workshop scheduled for the following day. She'd already taught her signature Pussy Gazing workshop to seventy-odd women inside one of the festival's biggest double tents. The next workshop was a new one called Sex Elevated, and it was based on the learnings we'd experienced as a couple in our own sex life and relationship. That very afternoon, another door was about to open.

Sex elevated

Over the previous three years, we'd gone subterranean on a self-created sexual healing journey. We didn't know that's what we were doing at the time; we thought we were saving our marriage by doing whatever we could to improve our intimacy and connection. We'd gone the way of most relationships: we'd started with red-hot intimacy, which eventually petered out into a barely-there sex life. This caused problems, resentment and an undercurrent of dissatisfaction that reared up between us on the regular. We made a loose decision before our daughter was born, and then a concrete one afterwards, to begin exploring this challenge in a meaningful way so that our relationship didn't dissolve at the hands of this sex chasm. We knew we weren't alone in this challenge, and yet it wasn't being talked about in a way that resonated with us or made us feel like we weren't somehow failing at this thing called a long-term relationship.

What we'd come to discover was that what was happening in the world when it came to sex was nothing short of catastrophic. Communication woes, resistance to authentic vulnerability, lack of presence, fear of being exposed, surface-level physical relating with no depth, the ramifications of trauma, lifestyle, religion and societal and familial constructs – sex was a mess in the lives of many. So after going from lacklustre humping where Flynn wanted it and Lacey didn't, to fully lit-up lovemaking where both of us felt desirous and satisfied, Lacey felt compelled to share what she'd learned with anyone interested.

She'd been on her own journey of healing since deciding to become a mother. After realising she had very negative views on motherhood, pregnancy and childbirth, she began diving deep into herself to understand the root cause and implications of these dark feelings. On her journey towards having an empowered birth, she began disentangling issues she'd faced around her body, her sexuality, confidence and self-trust. All of this would lead the way to a new direction in her career, where she'd begin teaching everything she'd learned around women's empowerment and sexual awakening through running an online group coaching programme, holding live workshops and via press and media features.

LACEY

I hadn't created much of a curriculum yet for that first Sex Elevated workshop. I spoke with the festival organisers and pitched it, and they were keen. I trusted that I'd figure out the scope once it was time to teach. I hadn't expressed it much, as I didn't want Flynn to feel pressure, but I had a deep desire for him to teach this alongside me. I knew he'd find it challenging: not because he wasn't capable, but because he had a strong view on who he was as a designer and artist, and doing this, teaching people about sex, would challenge that. I knew he'd somehow feel like a fraud – as if he wasn't someone who should be teaching people about sex. But I knew it would resonate. I thought if he shared his truth and everything he'd experienced and we'd learned together, it would be world-changing. So, I held a door open and asked. He said he'd think about. It was only an hour before the workshop when he said, 'Fuck it, let's do it.' My whole being ignited. I'm tearing up now remembering this. My husband was about to stand in front of dozens of people and talk for the first time about our sex life, the truth of what we went through, and ultimately how we healed it. Neither of us could have known then what would come. But we trusted and we jumped, together.

FLYNN

I was going through a major shift in my life and my perspective. I wanted a new direction to unfold, and I trusted it would when the time was right, even though that wasn't always easy. I never imagined it would come through working alongside Lacey, as the space of sexuality was her game, not mine. In that moment, the invitation from my dear Lacey was too good to knock back. I knew the time was right to try something new. I didn't have all the answers, but I knew if I shared my truth, it would all work out. So I said yes, and I dived in. If it wasn't for all the positive feedback I received, I might have just enjoyed it as a one-off. But people's genuine heart-felt thanks made me realise there was something in this work.

After the workshop, countless people came up to us and thanked us for sharing our truth alongside the tools we'd developed (some of which we'll share in this book). Men stayed to thank Flynn for being there and sharing the masculine side. Women stayed to thank him for being there to show what a connected, sexually conscious man looks and sounds like. He was a total hit. The workshop was a success and was the start of our career together as sex and relationship coaches and educators.

Who we are and who we're not

We're not trained professionals in the world of sex and relationships. We're not therapists, counsellors or doctors. We're not tantric practitioners or trained in any spiritual sexual practices.

Instead, we're a couple of over a decade with a penchant for coaching and guiding others through big life experiences. We have a knack and desire for digging deep, getting uncomfortable, making changes and sharing our findings with the world. We've both spent the better part of the last decade engaged in a variety of healing and self-development modalities, trainings and explorations. We met through yoga, created a meditation platform together for a hot minute, and both have a tendency towards being self-directed, autonomous beings who take ownership over our health, wellbeing and lives in general.

That's what this book does: it helps you take ownership of these things.

When we sat on national television in London to be interviewed about our runaway hit of a podcast, *Lacey & Flynn*

Have Sex, the presenter's first question to us was, 'What are your qualifications?'

Lacey answered: 'Our qualifications are that we're doing this work in our lives every day, so our students and the people who are tuning in know that we're showing up. We're showing up to our relationship, we're doing this work and we're coming from that humble place that this is real for us.' That's always been the case.

After that first workshop and seeing how many people were helped by us sharing our experiences, we felt a calling to continue with the work. Within a month of the festival, we began sharing videos online exploring our bold ideas: 'Have sex (even when you don't feel like it)', 'Penetration: is it pleasure or pain?' and 'Healing sexual trauma with sex', to name a few. In just five short weeks, our casual, unedited, one-take video lessons, which we shot in our home office while our daughter napped, had garnered around 160,000 views. We created a live online Sex Elevated course, and began teaching couples from around the world.

The following January, we launched our current self-paced Sex Elevated course, which has seen more than 4,500 couples and singles go through the lessons and practices we've developed.

A year later, in April 2021, we released our podcast, which skyrocketed our work's reach. It went to number one in the UK, alongside loads of other countries, and charted internationally. At the time of writing this, our show has been downloaded half a million times, we've created our own suite of products (visit laceyandflynn.com) and we've featured in our first TV documentary about the female orgasm, sharing Pussy Gazing and our pleasure over orgasm approach.

We've been told that what makes us different is our relatability, and that even when we're sharing things that are heavy, big or downright awkward, we somehow make it accessible, easy to grasp and fun. People also like that we don't hold anything back. In our podcast, for example, we've created an entirely new genre of sex education where we actually have sex live on air. It's not pornography or voyeurism. It's two consenting adults in a real long-term relationship, recording the raw and real truth of our sex life. We describe what's happening, we share our emotions, we laugh, we cry, and we show everyone who's listening and resonates with it that they're not alone. Ultimately, our mission is to create more sexually thriving individuals and relationships, and in sharing our sex, raw and uncensored, we've been able to do that in leaps and bounds.

'I just want to say how much of an impact your podcast has had on my relationship and sexual intimacy with my wife. We both listen at separate times and make notes, and we sit down once a week and talk about it. Now when we have sex, I feel so connected with her, not just physically but spiritually as well.'

David

What this book is – and what it isn't

This book isn't a how-to. It's not a one-two-three to better doggy, or a step-by-step guide on how to make her cum. Instead, it's a behind-the-scenes look at what's happening with sex, relationships and intimacy. It's everything we believe is at the core of living a sexually liberated life that's authentic and not performative. It's a full-throttled exploration into many facets of sexual relating and what we've discovered, personally and professionally, on our journey towards having and sharing deep, meaningful, elevated sex.

It's nuanced, it's bold, it's tender and it's real. In these pages, we've shared the truth of our lives, and sharing the truth is a value we hold dear. We believe in authenticity and in sharing the very experiences and medicines that have mended our own lives, in order, perhaps, to reach, relate to and assist others.

We give you guidance on practices you can do in your life straight away, and we also give you prompts for going deeper, either in conversation with your lover or on your own, pen-and-journal style. We also give you plenty to think about and feel into.

Our work is very much of the body. We believe the only way to restore harmony to humans relating and to liberate sexual expression the world over is to help people connect and tune in to their own bodies. This work can't just be talked about and mused over. It must be actioned, felt, unfolded through the very forms that are initiated when we come into sexual contact, either with ourselves solo or with another.

This book might challenge you. In fact, we hope it does. Growth can only really happen when we stretch outside our own comfort zones. It's in this new terrain that we challenge our limiting beliefs, storylines and preconceived notions about ourselves and the world. Ultimately, we want this book to point the way forward; a resource through which you learn how to have epic sex not because we give you a formula, but because we give you a roadmap back to your authentic and fully expressed sexual self.

Who this book is for – and who it's not for

This book is for individuals and couples, singles and partnered humans, who are open and ready to explore new vantage points from which to view and express their sexuality. We teach to those in relationships and those who are single, so regardless of your status in this field, you can benefit from and fully participate in the teachings and practices offered throughout these pages. The ultimate goal of this book is learning to move beyond surface-level shagging into deep, meaningful, elevated sex. It's about understanding all the things that get in the way of a person's fullest sexual expression, healing these and creating a more sexually expressive way forward that centres truth and pleasure. We're interested in the abolishment of shame and the redefining of what makes sex successful. We want to see a harmonising of feminine and masculine energies, and the unification of men and women, so that sexual dynamics become more satisfying and soulful for all involved.

If you've experienced any of these, this book is probably for you:

- a desire divide, where one partner wants it more than the other
- lack of turn-on, arousal or desire
- challenges communicating your needs and desires in the bedroom
- relationships that have ended because of a lack of intimacy and connection
- surface-level sex with no depth or spiritual connection
- fear of exposing yourself or being too vulnerable
- pain while having sex, or a feeling like you just can't be penetrated
- challenges feeling present or in the moment
- feeling like you're in your head and disconnected from your body
- feeling numb, like you don't have much sensation or feeling in your sexual centre
- fear around getting close, opening up or being seen by a lover
- shame around your genitals or body as a whole
- unresolved trauma that keeps you from sexual satisfaction
- the Rejection Loop, where one partner is always in pursuit and the other is always declining advances
- resentment in your relationship around sex or lack thereof
- challenges maintaining stamina in the bedroom
- an unsatisfying sexual dynamic

Truth be told, *Come Together* is not for the diehard sceptic. In these pages, you will be exploring a broader perspective on human existence. It's not dogmatic, but it isn't rational, logical or right-brained either – so if that's a no-go for you, turn back now. If you're easily offended and not willing to look at the roots of said offence, this probably isn't your bag. If you love political correctness and have a desire for everything to be tidy and fit into tight little boxes, put this down and run for your life (but then come back and read this, because you're probably not thriving in the bedroom).

But if you want to live your best life, fuck like a god/goddess and be your most expansive self, buckle up. We'll get on just fine. And listen: even if you're hesitant and a bit unsure, but you feel an inner calling to do this work and dive in, this is probably a good fit for you. We know a lot of our students, clients and listeners have that experience – they're keen, a bit excited and a *lot* nervous, and they find themselves on the edge of their seats with both enthusiasm and trepidation. Mixed and somewhat divergent feelings make sense when we're on the precipice of big explorations that challenge the status quo and how we've each been living our lives to date. This isn't a dealbreaker, though. Most of our clients who've experienced the biggest life transformations also once sat in that seat: the one that says 'I'm ready' and 'I want to run' at the same time.

Inclusivity, heteronormativity and repping the feminine and masculine

Since our work is first and foremost based on our personal experiences, we tend to resonate with people who are in similar relational dynamics: one man, one woman and cis-gendered. We are keen believers and espousers of ancient principles of feminine and masculine energy and dynamics, as opposed to new-school rhetoric regarding what makes a woman feminine or a man masculine. Instead, this is about the *essence* with which we each individually most align, and how that's experienced and expressed throughout our lives.

The feminine	The masculine
• being	• doing
• receiving	• planning
• feeling	• achieving
• creative	• logical-minded
• expressive	• focused
• intuitive	• goal-orientated
• slow	• fast
• inward	• outward

Your essence is the core of who you are. Most of the time, men align with masculine essence and women with feminine essence; however, it can be the opposite as well. In your daily life, you will dip in and out of masculine and feminine energies, no matter your essence, gender or sex. Each person will have their own unique balance of these two energies and usually a single core essence with which they most identify.

When a woman is feminine essence but spends the majority

of her time in her masculine energy, then, if she's in a hetero relationship, she'll probably have challenges in the bedroom.

The same things go for a masculine-essence man who spends the majority of his time in his feminine energy.

This is because our sexual expression and desire is interwoven with our core essence. This doesn't mean that any number of other configurations can't still have epic sex lives. In our experience, though, personally and professionally, we've seen time and time again that sexual difficulties arise when the core essence of a being isn't attended to, expressed or understood. When there's a dichotomy between the core essence and the energies we live in and act from, this often creates issues in the bedroom, because polarity is lost (more on this on page 53).

We each must reckon with our own essence and the balance of the feminine and masculine energies across our lives in order to have an elevated sex life. This is something we'll explore as the book unfolds.

In terms of sexual orientation, we've had queer couples love our work and hate our work. We've also had hetero couples love our work and hate our work. We've resonated with trans and non-binary people, and have also done the exact opposite. We explored going all-out inclusive for a stretch there, and ultimately realised we were doing a disservice – not only to the work, but also to our students.

Because we relate to the feminine (Lacey) and the masculine (Flynn), we believe our work is best suited to men and women who are cis-gender and probably in heterosexual relationships. Although this might mean our work isn't as relatable for some people as it is for others, we hope that what we lack in diversity, we make up for in integrity and honesty. We teach what we know – and there is plenty we don't know. We're happy for anyone from any walk of life to pick up our book and take from it what's right for them while leaving anything that isn't. At the end of the day, we've made a vow to share what's true for us with the intention that anyone who resonates with what we share can take from it what they may.

We value the lived experiences of those who are different to us, and we also have no interest in trying to convince you of anything. In fact, this book desires the opposite – to give you a new lens to try on so you can see the world for yourself. We're not your eyes. We're not you. We're Lacey and Flynn – two people out of billions on this earth. We can't speak for anyone but ourselves. So, we've chosen to go balls to the wall, poon to the moon, and say everything we think and feel, always from love and always with a desire to stand in our integrity.

Things we know very little about

We're very good when it comes to the energetics of sex and dis-ease born of emotional, spiritual challenges that then manifest physically as pain or discomfort. However, this book does not relieve you of the responsibility to seek out help if you have pain, and is not intended to replace the information given to you by a healthcare professional.

If you have unexplored trauma, this might not be the right place to start. It's often best to work through acute challenges or overdue stuff that's still impacting you in a 'held container' first. That being said, every person is unique, and perhaps reading some of these pages will help you. We leave it up to you to do what's right for you and we will be discussing unexplored trauma more on pages 74–9.

As you dive deeper into this work, you'll come to understand how sex can be the bridge that brings you closer instead of just the bridge you cross when you're already feeling close or 'in the mood' (and gosh, we can't wait to help you implode the concept of 'the mood' and teach you why you need to have sex even when you don't feel like it.)

Yes, this work might be confronting, and at times you might gasp incredulously at our sheer audacity. There's no problem with that. You can be aghast and then breathe through it, witnessing your own trigger points and then deciding if you're ready to explore, heal and dissolve them, or be controlled by them. That's your power, and we want you to take it: to own your life, heal the past and be the person you most want to be.

We're not here to uphold the status quo. We're here for a sexual revolution. One where people heal deeply, enjoy deep pleasure and become mature and expansive across all parts of life. We believe sex is the perfect ground for making this happen.

That being said, we've helped women move past vaginal pain and learn to get deeply fucked for the first time in their lives, and we've guided men to become powerhouse lovers with more mandurance than ever before. We've helped men and women alike heal sexual trauma, touch themselves for the first time and actually enjoy it, move beyond shame and develop deeply satisfying sex lives that far surpassed anything they'd previously encountered or imagined possible for themselves. We've helped women open up and let love in, we've helped men learn to fuck from the heart and we've assisted many people to overcome a variety of ailments manifesting in their sexual centres. It's nuanced, this world, and if you love the grey zone, then you're in luck – because that's where we spend most of our time.

How this book works

This book is broken down into twelve chapters that take you on a journey through the tenets of deep, meaningful, elevated sex. At once autobiography, manifesto and guide, this book will show you we've been there, done the work and come out the other side with some golden nuggets to help you on your path. There are stories and bits of feedback from students and clients throughout these pages to add further depth where appropriate. We've also each included our individual input at various intervals when we felt called to share a story in our own voices and from our unique perspectives. Since we're both coaches, you'll be asked powerful questions throughout the book and encouraged to reflect on them. Coaching is a modality that encourages the student or client to come to their own answers and conclusions. What you need is to think and feel for yourself. Sure, it can be important and worthwhile to get support. That's why you're here. And part of this support will be us asking you questions so you can go deeper into yourself and the journey towards elevated sex.

What is elevated sex?

Elevated sex weaves the whole human into the experience. Instead of being about a surface-level shag, elevated sex asks each lover to bring more of themselves into the experience.

Surface-level shag

- no emotional attunement
- little to no communication
- lacking soul or depth
- doesn't take both partners' needs into consideration
- disconnected
- goal-orientated
- orgasm reigns supreme
- mind- and thought-centred

Elevated sex

- emotionally attuned
- communication is key
- soulful and spiritual
- both partners are equally seen and revered
- connected
- present- and path-orientated
- pleasure and feeling reign supreme
- body- and soul-centred

We're also going to give you practices to do. Some will be solo and others will be partnered. If you don't have a partner, you can do these practices with a friend, or skip them until later down the road, or altogether. It goes without saying that the more you put into any pursuit, the more you'll get out of it. If you read these pages and don't do any of the embodied practices or reflections, you'll still learn loads and will probably have your sex life blown open in important ways. If you do the work, though, of bringing these practices and tools to life through action, you will see and experience changes on a deeper level. Ultimately, the choice is yours.

If you desire at any point to take this work to the next level, you can visit us at laceyandflynn.com, where you can join a programme, get coached or purchase goodies from our shop that will boost your sexual experience.

Come Together and the secret to deep, meaningful, elevated sex

It might seem odd that we've dedicated this book to our children. If it wasn't for our children, though, we wouldn't be here sharing this message with you. We're of the firm belief that children bring gifts with them when they come into this world. They're the ultimate creative manifestation – the perfect expression of the feminine and masculine weaving together to create something born of perfect union. You don't have to have kids to have soulful sex, but for us, their imperativeness to our work cannot be denied.

Our daughter brought the teachings with her. The gift of her life not only graced us with the preciousness of who she is as a person but also taught us both how to become more of who we each are. She brought sensuality, expressiveness and intimacy with her when she came into this world. Our son brought unification and vision. Through his arrival, we became a much stronger team and developed a mission that we never would have come to without him. He also brought the integrated masculine – the strong and heart-centred presence of a boy who knows who he is.

It is through our children that we have come together more than ever before: as individuals, perfectly aligning the self to the self, and as a couple, forging greater intimacy and a love born of a commitment to ourselves and one another.

The secret to deep, meaningful, elevated sex will probably be different for each and every one of us. But if you're anything like us, it will have something to do with being *all* of you. Showing yourself to yourself, letting yourself be seen by others and no longer hiding the bits of you that feel unworthy of the light. This is true intimacy: seeing yourself clearly and letting others do the same. The mess and perfection – it all belongs in elevated sex. The secret will probably also have something to do with depth, with letting yourself move below the surface into the deeper layers of your soul self and authentic sexual expression. From this place, you get to go beyond performance and pastiche into gorgeous, vulnerable, fuck-yes authenticity, where you're no longer afraid to desire, be desired and live the orgasmic life of your dreams.

1

Sex matters

Like us, you might have thought sex was a cherry on top of the relationship sundae. If it wasn't going well, it didn't matter so much, because the rest of the dessert was the most important bit. We came to learn, though, that the idea of sex as the cherry on top was a fallacy; instead, sex is better viewed as the bowl in which the whole relationship sundae sits. Sex matters, intimacy matters, and it's time to set the record straight on why sex and sensual intimacy are crucial for creating and maintaining a thriving relationship.

It wasn't easy for us to learn this lesson, and we hope to help you bypass some of the pitfalls we experienced.

The beginning

We started our relationship on a snowy winter's night in Berlin in 2010. Lacey was hosting a small Christmas gathering at her yoga studio in Kreuzberg, and although Flynn had yet to officially attend a class (he'd been cancelling regularly as he prepared for his first solo exhibition at a design gallery in Mitte), he had fellow Australian friends regularly attending. So, when the invite went out via email, he asked if he could come too.

At the time, Lacey was with a boyfriend, with whom she'd travelled from Canada, and Flynn was just out of a relationship with the girlfriend with whom he'd travelled over from Australia.

Yoga studio parties tend to just involve people sitting on the floor, listening to music and, in this case, drinking cheap wine from the Spätkauf around the corner. But Lacey was still a bit nervous-excited, delighted to be hosting a gathering at The Yoga Emporium, the space she'd created and was teaching at, which she was renting on her own.

Flynn arrived in a swirl of snow and with a knock on the door. When he tells this story, he always says that Lacey answered and was the loudest, most Canadian person he'd ever encountered. Even though she *didn't* say this, he insists she said, 'Welcome! What's your name? Hi, Flynn. Hey, everyone, let's give Flynn a big warm Canadian welcome,' in the most East Coast accent imaginable. She insists it was more like, 'Hey, you're Flynn? Welcome, come on in. Can I take your coat?' in an excited albeit normal pitch with an accent that was softening month by month with her new Euro lifestyle.

Neither of us was appraising one another romantically at this stage. Lacey's boyfriend was there, and Flynn was busy chatting with mutual friends. But there was something between us. A spark of recognition, maybe. Lacey looked at Flynn more than a few times, trying to figure him out. With his full head of long dark curls and finely manicured moustache, she wondered whether it was all ironic or if he was as he appeared – beautiful, different, interesting. Flynn was curious about Lacey; he liked her name and cheeky grin, and the way she moved elegantly through the space. But he knew she was already with someone else, and didn't give it a second thought.

There just happened to be a photographer at the party that night, a woman who was making a book about the businesses and lives of people on Wranglestraße (the street the studio was on). She captured the party prep, the party in full swing (if it ever hit that stage), and pictures of both of us at different intervals, talking to friends and listening in on the same conversations.

Two days later, Flynn finally came to a yoga class. The photographer happened to arrive at the end to do a solo shoot with Lacey, and captured the first photo of just the two of us. The heavy wool curtain that separated the teaching space from the draughty front door had come down. Flynn, being quite tall, was standing and pinning part of the curtain back into place, while Lacey stood on a ladder next to him, pinning up another part of the Turkish market-bought fabric.

In the photos, Flynn's wearing his winter jacket and one shoe, with a bare foot on the other side. Half there, half out the door, and with his hands fully present, high up and helping. There are two snaps: one where Lacey's doing the curtain, and another where she's looking back over her shoulder at the camera.

Before Flynn left, he asked Lacey about the studio. 'You're doing this on your own?' he enquired.

'I borrowed some money from my dad, but yeah, it's just me here.'

'And you found the space, and started it all on your own?'

'I did,' Lacey replied.

His eyes were warm and impressed. She felt seen in her efforts for the first time. There was a recognition there, and something happened in that moment: kindred spirits found one another in a glance, in the cool draught of the doorway, piecing the makeshift space back together.

The following year, Flynn came to a couple more classes. Lacey eventually left the studio and started teaching out of the spare room in her flat to save money. After one class, in the doorway of her home, Flynn invited Lacey to attend his design exhibition, which he'd been working towards for the better part of a year. Mutual friends would be there. She said yes, but didn't make it until the *finissage* – the closing night party.

Lacey travelled to Mitte on the U-Bahn train with a shared friend, a student from the studio who was also part of Flynn's expat posse. Lacey remembers stepping from the street into the gallery and immediately feeling emotional. Around the room, on white plinths, were eight or ten large glass spheres of light, all in different colours, balancing on shiny brass bases. The room was full of people. There was no other light save for these glowing spheres, each of which was half illuminated and half not. Kind of like phases of the moon.

---------- 6 ----------

LACEY

I immediately fell in love with Flynn. I didn't know him, but I loved him. I loved the soul that had imagined this work and made it real. I loved the magic of it, the high-calibre luxury and design. It felt like him made manifest in a material object. I felt his spirit, his potential, his essence, in the lights (called X&Y) and in the gathered swarm of people there to celebrate the art.

He came to meet me and showed me how the lights worked. Rotating the lights changed their brightness and colour. You could literally swirl the heavy glass spheres in your hands, rotating them on their bases, and the light would change with the angles. He'd designed these objects and worked painstakingly with a German manufacturer to make them a reality. He blew my mind and heart – I think because I'd finally met someone who dreamed and made their dreams a reality, who was entrepreneurial like me. It was magic.

FLYNN

I was thrilled when I saw her at the door. The exhibition had been running for weeks and she'd finally come. I felt like a male bower bird who had created the most beautiful space he could in order to wow his ideal mate. Luckily for me, it worked.

———————————————— **,** ————————————————

We went on to become lovers and partners quite quickly after that. We travelled to Sweden to deliver one of his lights to a client, and shacked up in Lacey's Kreuzberg flat before signing a lease on a place of our own, which happened to be on Wranglestraße, the very street we'd met on.

In the beginning, our sex was wild and primal. It was that all-consuming sex where thoughts don't stand a chance and everything is lusty and bodied, all flesh and hearts and sweat. We had sex often, every day, sometimes multiple times. Our biggest issue was dragging ourselves from the flat to find food and coffee, or to do work here and there.

There are loads of other details that would be fun to share – like Beer Pyramid and May Day in Görlotizer Park or bike rides under the falling cherry blossoms – but in service to sex and the importance thereof, we won't digress into nostalgia.

It's important to note that we were in love and both very clear we'd be together forever. It was barely ever a question, the trajectory of our relationship. This was the meeting of two souls who had travelled from their respective continents to find one another in Berlin.

But after a few years, challenges arose in our sex life.

It became a game of cat and mouse, or what we coined 'the Rejection Loop', which we'll explain in full in the next chapter. At first, there were simple excuses, like being tired or too busy, or not being in the mood, but then these reasons never seemed to shift. There was always something that kept Lacey from wanting to connect physically. It wasn't that she didn't love Flynn, or find him attractive or enjoy closeness; it was something else that she didn't have words for or an understanding of. This lack of self-awareness and comprehension made the experience frustrating, and we found ourselves irritated with one another, not fully knowing how to claim our feelings or experiences. We were at the start of our sexual healing journey, and so weren't yet versed in conscious communication or holding space. Instead, we were frustrated, lashing out and unsure of how to navigate the whole ordeal.

LACEY

I'd never been in a relationship or witnessed one where sex and intimacy stood the test of time. I was under the impression that this was simply the natural order. You're hot and lusty to start with, and then you become besties who hang out and enjoy life together, with very little intimacy. This had been the way of my parents, who broke up because of a lack of intimacy and sex. And it was what I saw all around me in everyone else's relationships, too. I didn't realise it was a problem. So, when Flynn made it out to be, I was caught off guard.

FLYNN

A slowly fading sex life was not something I could tolerate. If Lacey was the one for me, if I had travelled so far and been through past heartaches to find her, I needed the sex to work, too. For me, it was a key component of a thriving relationship. It was non-negotiable. So, I stood my ground. Looking back now as I write this, I'm glad I felt this way. Because it set the stage for the whole beautiful journey we went on to heal our sex life and ultimately heal the sex lives of many others in the process.

9

The middle

Lacey didn't want to admit the importance of sex in a relationship. She wanted the rest of the relationship to be enough, but for Flynn, it wasn't (and in the end, it wasn't enough for her, either, but it took hindsight to truly understand this). This situation – Flynn wanting it and Lacey not wanting it – created a lot of tension, arguments and challenges.

We found ourselves, for a number of years, with a great relationship save for this huge, gaping hole of intimacy, sex and, ultimately, the fullest expression of love.

Flynn resented Lacey for not wanting to be with him, and Lacey resented Flynn for making sex such a big deal.

FLYNN

We never talked about breaking up, but the lack of sex impacted other parts of our relationship. It was a dark spot that seemed to spread. There was resentment, sure, but underneath that was sadness. Neither of us felt understood by the other, but ultimately, we didn't fully understand ourselves yet.

We began to consciously mend our sex life when we were expecting our first child. Lacey began a self-guided journey of getting to know her body in new ways, and through this, she started to heal her relationships with sex, desire, her body and the fear she had around intimacy, opening up and letting go.

We'd never expected that birth would slingshot our sex life, but it showed us the depths of the chasm we'd been experiencing. At first, Lacey wanted the postpartum period to buy her a good six to twelve months of sex-free time. At about the five-month mark, things got very tense. We'd had sex a few times, but the separateness and lack of closeness between us had become stark. It was a breaking point – and one of the best things to happen to us.

This is when we decided to dive into our sex instead of skirting around it forever. We'll spend the rest of the book unfolding this journey and all the lessons it gave us, but for now, we want you to see that we didn't have this figured out from the start.

No matter where you are on your journey towards ele-vated sex – the process and practice of centring sex and intimacy, making it soulful, and prioritising the healing and pleasure of both partners – we get it. We've been at the start, we've navigated the middle and we've come out the other side. We're not at the end by any means – we don't think there *is* an end to this work – but after years of deliberate attention and devotion, we're at a place where our love life is thriving.

After a sex session, we often say, 'That was the best sex we've ever had,' and it's not because we're spring chick-ens rocking the honeymoon phase. We're parents, we run businesses, we're at the cusp of middle age (well, truth be told, Flynn's already there), and yet we have sex more often – and with more passion, lust, depth and intimacy – than either of us did in our younger years.

It's a con to believe sex is for the young. Sex is for everyone, if you want it to be. Every person is sexual. What you might not be is sexually expressive. You might feel disconnected from your sexuality, but that doesn't negate your innate sex-uality. We all come from sex. It's the core energy that made us manifest in this world. Thus, it is a part of who we are. How we express it is up to each of us. Whether you stay awkward or ashamed, numb or overwrought – that's up to you.

And we don't say that to be harsh; we say that to excite you. You are powerful. You get to choose how you write your sexual story from here on out (which we'll help you with in chapter four). The way it's been is not the way it has to be. Trust us: if the past was destined to be the future, we'd be two dried up and sexless raisins, quietly despising one another, trying to go about our day-to-day lives while screaming deep down, wishing we could both just be free to love, be wild and be our most expressed juicy selves.

Because that's what elevated sex afforded us – the chance to let our fullest selves be expressed. Our emotions, our desires, our souls and our funny humanity. Sex isn't a place just for the flirty; it's a place where all of you can come to be witnessed and expressed. We've learned that sex isn't the place to come to when everything is just dandy in life. It's the place we come no matter how we are and no matter what's happening. It's the full stop, the ellipses, the run-on sentence that never seems to end. It can be any part of the story – and the story you write now is up to you.

Sex: the great healer

What would your life be like if you could bring all of you to sex? Your sadness and enthusiasm, your awkwardness and fury. What would it be like to be self-possessed and in full ownership of yourself so that you could articulate it between the sheets, solo or with a partner?

It's worthwhile considering the above, because it's common to think that only the *best* of us belongs in sex. But what about the *rest* of us? Why can't we love ourselves and be loved in our fullness?

We used to think sex was for being sexy – and it is. But that's just one dimension. It's also for primal guttural roars, weepy eyes and snotty faces, uproarious laughter, grief-processing, tender holding and every other expression of self that one can muster.

We don't need to save sex for when we're polished, sassy and at our 'best'. Sex can be the healing ground where we allow parts of ourselves to come through that we might otherwise keep tucked away from the rest of life. Our desire is to teach you this and show you how in the pages that follow.

Imagine if sex, the act of expressing your body and soul's desires, became fertile ground for your own deliverance. Imagine if you discovered who you are, what you want and why you're here – all through the expression of your sexuality.

'I can't believe the changes, just from having sex! I'm more confident, I'm way happier and I've actually been able to create a new position for myself at work. My relationships are better – with myself, my husband, co-workers and pretty much everyone I encounter. I feel like I'm just now coming alive.'

Holly (34)

Let's take it a step further. We want you to really picture this . . .

You arrive to a sex session with your partner. You're both deeply connected to yourselves. There's no body shame holding you back or unspoken resentment muddying the space. You both know who you are, and you know one another, too. You see one another clearly and you respect each other, not as you'd like the other to be, but as they are in this moment – perfect, present, soulful and human. You choose to show love, to express the depths of yourself, through intimacy. You're no longer afraid of feeling, or of sharing your feelings with someone else. You can clearly express your desires, thoughts, fears and ecstasy. You're comfortable both giving and receiving love, and the things that held you back from showing up fully in the past are a long-distant memory. Now, you're here in full presence. You know your body is capable of infinite pleasure, and you feel worthy and allowed to go there. When you give to your partner, you're no longer bypassing your own needs, and when you receive, you do it with an open heart, happy to bask in the love and adoration. You know you don't have to be anything other than the way you are, so there's no per-formance, just truth. And through this truth, you make love. You leave behind the need to think and instead, you feel. You enter into the full expanse of your body and you learn new depths of orgasmic bliss. The deeper you go, the more open you are to yourself, your partner, pleasure and love.

Through this connection to your full self, to another and to intimacy, your whole life opens up. How could it not?

It's exciting, to completely rewrite the purpose and function of sex. We're not doing it from a cognitive place, though, one where we've decided that this is what sex ought to be. Instead, we're unpicking the indoctrination that says sex is x, y, z, and instead we're allowing the innermost truth of sex to be revealed from within.

That's the elevated sex difference. It's no longer about someone telling you or you seeing it and then embodying it as gospel. It's now about learning from within and letting your own experiences and insight guide you.

That's why this calibre of truly connected sex has the capacity to blow open every facet of life. It's not about jack-rabbiting to scratch a recurring itch. It's much deeper than that. Sure, you'll still be sated on a sexual, primal level. You can blow your load, have a cum, pass out and be a total primate. That's welcome here. And you can also go deeper into your soul. Into the part of you that longs for connection and true intimacy, that wants to feel love, to let go and dance in an expanse of ecstasy and devotion.

You can heal the past, sink into the present and align to your future – all through sex, sexual energy and self-pleasure. You can use your genitals, your good old-fashioned pussy or cock (we'll get into language later, so don't run yet), as a GPS, guiding you both deeper into yourself and further along your life path.

It's powerful, healing stuff, and we're very excited to share it with you.

Going solo

You don't need a partner at all; you can do this solo. In fact, the work we do and what we teach is about you first and the relationship second. Ultimately, we each need to come into ourselves before someone else can come into us; from this place, we fully align and can come together. We need to understand ourselves first, to love ourselves and become the captains of our own soul and body ships. This is the first step – and, because it's not linear, it's also the ongoing dedication of this work.

You first, the relationship second. Rinse and repeat in both directions.

That being said, you can do this work on yourself and your relationship at the same time. If you're reading this solo and you're single, do the work on yourself. If you're reading this solo and you're in a relationship, do the work on yourself and bring it to your lover to do too. If your person isn't interested just yet, focus on yourself. You have no excuses. The only reason not to do it is because you truly don't want to. Or maybe you're not at a place yet in your journey where you're ready for it – and that's fine. We all have to walk our own unique paths and be true to what's right for each and every one of us.

There's a delicate and juicy space between readiness and not being ready, between comfort and discomfort, and we love to hang out in this fertile land. Being uncomfortable is not a problem. If you feel awkward or ashamed, unsure or stuck, all of that is okay here. You don't need to be raring to go (although hell yes if you are). You can have trepidation and still turn the pages and unfold the journey.

Basically, who you are, how you are, where you come from and what you're currently feeling is perfect. You don't need to be at a certain stage in the journey to benefit. As long as you're open, you'll benefit from this work.

The importance of sex

As we have said, the idea that sex is some sort of cherry on top is wrong. It's the foundation of life, the very core of our existence, and it warrants far more attention than being the thing we do haphazardly at the end of the day when we're tired, worn out and don't have much to give.

We've all gone on for long enough disregarding sex, being immature about it, throwing it around casually, diminishing it, feeling ashamed of it and feeling out of control or lacking confidence around it. It's time that ends – and it changes with us.

The next generation deserves a life free from sexual shame. Heck, we deserve that. It doesn't even make sense that we have sexual shame to be begin with. Sex is an act of evolution, and yet we feel such discomfort around the very energy and action that propagates our species. It's a whack world that can't handle sex and surprise; we live in that place right now.

But you're a change-maker, aren't you? Either in big, dramatic sweeps or small daily gestures, you have a desire to awaken.

Sex means life. It means pleasure. And it also means power. But not the kind of power that's held over another. No, this power is embodied and can come from nowhere else but within, guiding the governor of said power into the fullest expression of themselves. This is the kind of power beholden to a sexually elevated society and world, the type we're creating through these pages and through you.

Sex has been used to diminish, inflict pain on, subjugate, disembody and silence people for eons. It's been commodified, commercialised and altogether taken from the true and authentic to the parody and performative. Grown men smirk and make sex jokes because they can't handle intimacy and are not truly embodied in their sexual expressiveness, and women freeze because they're afraid of what sex will do to them, or what it might mean if they were desirous beings made for more than simply being desired.

We have a problem here. Can you see it?

Don't you find it magnificently odd that this natural act could be used and twisted in such a way as to completely pervert the way we relate to it and do it? We think so. In fact, it's blown our minds so much that we've dedicated our lives to understanding and healing these very issues.

Sex isn't inherently challenging, shameful, problematic or distressing. It's the storylines and narratives that propagate and perpetuate these ways of being that aren't in service to our shared rising. The only thing this sexual illusion does is set each of us on the path of feeling lesser than we are. It keeps us afraid of our bodies, ashamed of our pleasure, scared of opening up too much or giving too deeply. It keeps us numb, on edge and never satisfied on a soul level. In fact, it keeps us severed from our souls, so that we don't even know there's more to it all than meets the eye.

But there's a feeling inside, and that's why you're here. You want to know how sex can illuminate your whole life, bringing you the deepest healing imaginable from all that ails you, while simultaneously offering you pleasure that was previously unimaginable.

We know these are some big claims. But since sex is the start of life, why not return there as the breeding ground for our own deliverance? Why not use this act – this basic, human, primal act – to emancipate ourselves from the bullshit of our time?

We believe that everything rises and descends from sex. If we free our sex, we free every other part of life – and we've seen it happen, in our own lives and in the lives of our students, clients, listeners and community. Please know, though, this isn't a singular healing gesture that happens all at once. It's more like a path that you decide to walk, and from here you get a different view, a new vantage point, from which to experience and witness your reality.

It's a calling – a calling to return to source via our bodies. A calling beyond esoteric ideology into the very fleshy realm of the human form. It's about healing your life by full-circling back to the start so that you can reconnect to the energy that made you, learning finally how to harness it. It's not about domination (although you might like that sometimes); instead, it's about integration and then right action. It's about taking the floating ghost of sex out of the haunted corner of life, seeing that it's not a ghost at all and then inviting this glorious light back into our hearts and loins.

Your sexuality is not a problem. You are not a problem. Your body is not a problem. You might have some problems to mend associated with distortions that you've begun to embody and live out as natural. But ultimately, at your core – your trusty and trustworthy self – you're a perfect being, ready to move into limitless potential by fucking yourself whole.

A new dawn

The day of empty sex has dawned.

It's time to co-create a reality where we all turn into sex, into intimacy and into relationships, with ourselves and others. It's the wounded one who runs from closeness. It's the awakening and healing one who seeks solace, comfort and love in the arms of proximity. This closeness we speak of is with the self and with those with whom we align. It's not about victimhood or being coddled; instead, it's about moving beyond the pain of 'every man for themselves' into a state of connection and care where we hold ourselves – and we hold one another – with respect, reverence and love.

To be honest, we're tired of broken relationships, broken homes and endings because individuals never got to know themselves to begin with, and so couldn't share who they really were with another being. We believe it is time for the rising of union. That doesn't mean you're inferior if you're single. It doesn't mean you find wholeness through the arms of another. What it means, is that if you desire true partnership and union, it's done from a place of wholeness in yourself first. It means that when things get tough, you learn to turn *into* the love you're cultivating instead of running away from it. It's about honest communication, mature individuals and a healing world where families and communities are restored.

Yes, we're idealists. We're also visionaries.

We see what wants to come forward in the world and what would ultimately enrich the lives of every person.

Nobody loses when we're each dedicated to our own rising and the shared elevation of each person; when we're open to learning, trying and embracing our humanity while holding space for the soul self. Everybody wins when we heal our toxicity around sex and sexuality. It's a big vision, and one that perhaps you'll share as you navigate these pages and understand the implications of sex on your life.

Sex is the answer. Now it's time to ask all the right questions.

Sex matters, distilled

- Sex truly matters; it isn't just the cherry on top of the relationship sundae.
- Sex can be used to heal and connect more deeply in the relationship, and isn't only for the hot and sexy moments when you feel your best.
- You don't need to be in a relationship to do this work; in fact, much of what we teach is best done solo first.
- It's essential to question the importance of sex in your life and what sex means to you.

2

The issue with sex in long-term relationships

Picture this: woman meets man, man meets woman. The chemistry is undeniable. The passion, blazing. They're completely enamoured with one another. Every glance is charged with desire. Each touch is teeming with the promise of intimacy and love. When they finally get naked, they're both ravenous for one another, blinded by an insatiable need for one another's bodies. It's electric. It's alive. It's deeply satisfying. When they're not together, they dream of being together. The magnetic pull between them makes it nearly impossible to do anything else but be together or think of one another. They're sure it will last for ever. How could it not? It's so extraordinary, so special.

And yet ... it doesn't.

At some point, whether six months down the line or two years in, it fades. Not the relationship, but this blinding, magnetic need for one another. The attraction, the hunger for sex, intimacy and proximity that marked the beginning of this love affair for the ages, dwindles, dissolves and evaporates. What remains in the wake of this sexual crescendo is something much less effervescent and exciting, which could be experienced as a lack, a nothingness. No lust, no insatiable desire, no daytime romps or midnight rendez-vouses. All the previous passion and fire has been replaced with a tepidness, an uninvited and undesired interloper: the cuddly-couch, Netflix-special warmth and affection of two familiar partners who love one another but aren't *hungry* for one another. Spontaneous and irrepressible sexual mag-netism have been replaced with not-very-often obligatory sex to satisfy the tally. But where's the fire? The sexual pizazz? The riding into the sunset bareback on a writhing unicorn made of orgasmic bliss?

Where's the hot-hot-heat that set this relationship ablaze to begin with? And will it ever return?

The answer is no – no, it won't. The honeymoon phase, the initial spark that promises couples the sexual moon, almost always, in the end, disappoints in its inevitable finiteness. And that's okay. It's not a failing; it's the natural trajectory of a relationship coming into being as the literal chemistry wears off. The honeymoon phase was never meant to last. It was meant to be the spark that ignited the relationship, not the kindling and fodder responsible for the relationship's longevity.

The problem is, though, that for most, the sex, intimacy and connection of the honeymoon phase is the pinnacle of the relationship, and then couples spend the rest of their lives together idealising this chapter. In addition, most people lack an understanding of what it takes to create a thriving sexual dynamic that, like a fine Cheddar, matures and gets better with time. Instead of seeing the honeymoon phase and subsequent long-term dynamic unfolding for what it is – the natural evolution of a relationship – couples see a shortcoming: that they are unable to maintain the early passion they both delighted in at the outset of the relationship.

This is what we'll call sexual stuntedness and many people stay in this stage for the rest of their lives. The relationship could last decades, and yet the couple might never sexually mature beyond the peak of the honeymoon phase. They might spend the rest of their lives recounting the good old days, back when they first met and they couldn't keep their hands off one another. They'll jointly and separately wish they could get back to that point, when they were younger, carefree, horny and fully enamoured with one another.

The honeymoon phase

The truth is, though, that the honeymoon phase is the adolescence of the sexual relationship. It's not mature, refined, developed or experienced. It's a significant part of the journey, but it's not the whole thing, and getting fixated on this point is like spending your whole life pining after your teen years. There's an entire sexual life to be had, and in order to let that unfold, you have to let go of what you see as your heyday and invite in the possibility that the best is yet to come. But it's going to take some work, and this is where you get to decide whether creating the elevated sex life of your dreams is a worthwhile endeavour (we imagine you think it is; why else would you be reading this book?).

If the honeymoon phase was a proper indicator of what a couple might expect from their sexual relationship, this book probably wouldn't be necessary. Too often, it seems that this initial stage, which many couples tout as hot, heavy and connected, has no real bearing on what will actually unfold in the long run for a couple in the bedroom. The truth is that this starting point ends up being a romanticised goal for many couples: a point to which they long to return when the lustre of fresh courtship wears off and the long-term relationship takes hold. However, we're here to set the record straight on the honeymoon phase and help you set a new bar for yourself that isn't reliant on going back in time to the point in your relationship where it all began.

What is it about the honeymoon phase that's so easily placed on a pedestal? After our own sex life died in the ass (this isn't an anal reference), we found ourselves pining after our courtship days, which had the added glamour of a European love affair. But besides the Euro dazzle, it was a standard honeymoon phase scenario that we both desperately wanted to resuscitate once it stopped pulsating with any hint of life.

Looking back, our honeymoon phase wasn't nearly as robust, expressive or epic as we thought it was at the time. It's only hindsight that offers this vantage point, but during those early days, Lacey wasn't fully able to articulate her desires and often went along with things, while Flynn didn't know how to be soulful in his delivery and had a penchant towards ego trips. The honeymoon phase that we once held in such high regard wasn't actually the joyride we thought it was. When we encourage our students and clients to look more deeply at this, they often discover the same thing. There's a blindness during this chapter of the relationship. The fire is so bright, it makes it hard to see subtleties, and we lose the textures in favour of broad strokes.

Truth be told, on the other side of our honeymoon phase, we thought there was something wrong with us. Even though we were both seasoned in the dating and relationship realms, we couldn't conceive of the idea of us getting it so wrong as to go from having a sexually charged and thriving relationship to one where there was nearly no sex at all. We'd both done this dance before, having had past partners where things had gone exactly same way. But with one another, with this love, we were sure it had to be different. We were sold on one another, and knew we were going to make a lifelong relationship out of this. If that was the case though, then why had things fizzled out sexually?

We didn't know what to do – so we didn't do anything.

We let the natural unfolding take place and we resented both the situation and one another. We were of the belief that relationships shouldn't need work, especially sexual relationships – and if they *did* need work, well, then they weren't really meant to be. This is the unfortunate running narrative in our culture, and it's obviously completely flawed. So instead of doing anything about our challenges, we let them run their natural course, and we spent time both together and privately begrudging the situation and one another, and idealising the honeymoon days, wondering how we could get back to that shiny time.

If this sounds familiar, it's because this is the same trajectory most couples find themselves on in their relationship. Couples aren't armoured with an understanding of the stages of a relationship, and don't understand that an elevated sex life actually requires a good amount of consistent individual and partnered work, because, ultimately, what you're up against is all your own habits, unprocessed baggage and a society that gets it all wrong when it comes to sex and relating (no biggie). We're taught to believe that only failed and failing relationships need work, and so when things start requiring maintenance, we take that as a catastrophic display of warning flares instead of being representative of what it actually takes to create a thriving partnership.

Think about it this way: most of us are happy to take our functioning car to a mechanic when a rattle starts to come from the engine bay, so why wouldn't we do that with a relationship – something that's far more important than any car?

Take a moment and look around your own life – from fictional relationships on the screen to the very real ones you witness or experience every day. Where are the thriving, mature, sexually charged relationships to be found? Are you in one? Do you know anyone in one? Have you ever witnessed one? If you're shaking your head no, we're not surprised. And if you're nodding your head yes, then you're in the minority.

Relationships built on authenticity, maturity, shared values, and a dedication to self-expression and self-development, where sexual thriving and intimate communication take centre stage, scarcely exist. But before you get desperately depressed by the tragedy of it all, let's do a 180 and get excited about the dawning of the age of the sexually expressed couple.

The sexual detective

In order for you to fully embrace your sexual potential, both solo and in partnership, you're going to have to become a fully-fledged sexual detective. You're going to need to understand all the ways in which you've been holding yourself back – in life and in relationships – from pleasure, intimate communication and mutual sexual thriving. In order to do this, you have to understand the repercussions of sexual disfunction and all the ways in which sexual disfunction manifests in relationships. When we say 'disfunction' here, we're not talking about physical challenges as the starting point; we're talking about emotional and spiritual challenges that then manifest on the physical plane.

When our sex life all but disappeared, it was as if a lifetime of sexual challenges that had been swept under the rug finally wouldn't stay hidden. For Lacey, sexual discomfort and issues with penetration that she'd managed to avoid facing now reared up and wouldn't go away. The honeymoon phase was so potent in its excitement and juiciness that she'd forgotten all her problems with sex: problems that she didn't even classify as problems, but that always unfolded in the same way no matter where in the world she was or who in the world she was with.

———————————— **6** ————————————

LACEY

It's only in looking back over my whole sexual life now that I can see the patterns emerge. I'd be fully turned on, open and sexually willing during the early stages of the relationship, and then when the excitement wore off, I'd start cliffhanging on the edge of the bed, hoping my partner at the time would think I was sleeping and leave me alone. Sex was enjoyable during the honeymoon phase because I was so wrapped up and in the moment, and this alone was enough for me to forget my sexual woes: was penetration pleasurable or painful? Was sex about my enjoyment or was it more about what I could give to my partner? Was I being true to myself or was I per-forming? These were questions I was asking myself without actually asking. I was conflicted, but I could forget the conflict when the relationship was fresh and just coming into being; however, once it was established, the conflict that had shifted to the background made its way back to the foreground to be seen and felt.

FLYNN

I was firmly in the camp that if the sex worked well, the relationship would probably work well. With Lacey, it was the best I had ever had. And she thought the same about me. We knew we had each met our match and that we were going to always be together. That's why it was so painful when the honeymoon phase wore off. I had been through relationships in the past where the sex was good and then it wasn't, and they all ended. I couldn't believe it was happening again with Lacey, because I desperately wanted it to work. I was convinced this time it would be different. I had no roadmap to follow and therefore I was lost and hurting inside.

———————————————— 9 ————————————————

From honeymoon phase to long-term relationship

So, there we were. Honeymoon phase done and dusted, with a new energy and chapter emerging: the long-term relationship. A long-term relationship is the perfect breeding ground for fostering a sexless dynamic. Because elevated sex requires presence, and most people aren't present or connected in their daily lives – to themselves or to one another – it's no wonder that most couples aren't having much sex, let alone sex that's soulful and satisfying. And because most people don't have a sexual lexicon for understanding what's transpiring individually or together, couples are left without the words or skills to communicate what's happening. In addition, sexual inadequacies and dissatisfaction that were overlooked because of the lustre of the honeymoon phase will come to the fore when the sheen of those early days wears off.

This is most true for women. Since most women have experienced some level of sexual repression – showing up sexually to satisfy their male partners, unsure of what they truly want in the bedroom, confused about how to enjoy themselves while balancing their partner's desires (which they've probably prized above their for own their entire sexual lives) – sex can feel like a minefield they're not equipped to handle. In our experience working with people who resonate with the scenario we've gone through, we usually see women who have little to no desire in sex because sex has scarcely been about them. They don't know who they are or what they want sexually, and they're tired of performing and having sex that dances on the line between pleasure and pain. They're tired of being jack-rabbited with very little sexual nuance to account for their pleasure, and so they shut down and shut out sex – sometimes entirely.

On the other hand, the men are still desiring sex: to connect with their partner, yes, but more to scratch the itch of horn-iness in an act that also offers a momentary experience of freedom, mind obliteration and satiation. They're not usually thinking about the calibre of sex they're having; they just want to have sex. Generally, they would like to be having more playful, adventurous sex but at this stage, with sex petering out and barely on the table, they take what they can get, slowly lowering the bar as the years go by. And from this place, we have the perfect opportunity for the Rejection Loop to be born and take hold.

What does sexual repression look like in women and men?

Women

- showing up sexually to satisfy their male partners
- being unsure of what they truly want in the bedroom
- feeling confused about how to enjoy themselves while balancing their partner's desires

- having little to no desire in sex because sex has scarcely been about them
- performing and having sex that dances on the line between pleasure and pain

Men

- only using sex to scratch the itch of horniness
- being goal-orientated towards the orgasm so they can momentarily let go
- feeling disempowered around how to pleasure and satisfy their partner
- being scared to communicate or share their deepest desires for fear of being less 'manly'
- not usually thinking about the calibre of sex they're having

Polarity

Let's talk for a minute about polarity and the spark that drew you and your partner together in the first place. Polarity is the powerful attraction that you both felt at the beginning of your relationship: an attraction strong enough that you changed your lives in many ways to be together. This phenomenon is the dance of having two opposite energies that magnetise one another. This experience of polarity is found in hetero and queer relationships alike. We can see men and women – or, more to the point, masculinity and femininity – as poles. A sure-fire attraction killer in a long-term relationship is a lack of polarity. It is why most long-term relationships break down. Just imagine two magnets pushed together with the same poles touch-ing. You can't quite get them connected; they fight one another, and there's a natural and powerful repulsion. On the other hand, when the magnets are turned around, with the opposite poles facing one another, there's a natural and powerful attraction that brings them easily together. It's the same with electricity. Negative and positive are opposing forces that play off each other to generate real power. Again, this isn't about gender or sex. It's about the core essence of a person, which is, more often than not, either masculine or feminine.

There's an idea that if you continue to do what you did at the beginning of your relationship, there will be no end. For many of us, we get comfortable, and we start to lose our edge, our pole, and therefore become less attractive to our partners. We stop putting effort into ourselves and into the relationship. We stop planning dates, exciting trips and surprises. Our boundaries soften, and much of life gets muddy in this middle ground where our own needs and our partners' needs aren't being fully met. This is a down-ward spiral to watch out for. Working to maintain your core pole is crucial when it comes to keeping the spark alive in your relationship. A lack of polarity is very damaging to a relationship, but it can be reversed with a clear understand-ing of what's going on and where new effort and focus needs to be.

Some questions to explore around polarity

- Do you align more with a feminine or masculine core essence?

- What activities or ways of being help to anchor you in your femininity or masculinity?
- Are there certain things that enhance or, alternatively, diminish the polarity in your relationship?
- How can you sit more firmly in yourself and create stronger polarity in your love life?

The chasm

'We've got to build a sex bridge and fuck our way across it,' one of us said, in no uncertain terms. A way less wet version of Niagara Falls had divided us, and we knew that the only way to mend this gaping divide was to get our sex on. Instead of waiting to feel connected to have sex, though, we had to use sex as the act that would bring us back into connection.

This is one of the key differences in an elevated sex practice – sex is used as the tool to foster a soulful connection and create healing and pleasure. Everything doesn't need to be golden in order to have said sex; in fact, choosing to have sex in the face of less-than-ideal circumstances is an imperative component of creating a thriving sex life where both partners want it.

Because, let's get real: you can't fix a sexual chasm by waiting to want to have sex. What you can do is reframe the type of sex you have for this next chapter.

Looking back at one of the earliest versions of our live online course, Sex Elevated, one couple literally had a chasm between them. As we all began, they were sitting as far apart as they could on the sofa while still remaining in the frame. There was a distance between them – physically and emotionally – and it was palpable. Full credit to them, they were there, fully showing up for this work, and their body language told a deep story. After working through the programme, and on the final call, they were sitting side by side, attached at the hip. The chasm had been bridged and they'd used sex, intimacy, communication and a soulful connection in order to begin the healing process and find their way to back to each other.

But, you might wonder, how can you have sex when you feel so disconnected? Don't you need to feel connected in the first place for sex to work?

As we'll address again and again throughout these pages, sex is no longer an action taken when everything perfectly aligns in life. That method of relying on a shared mood (and factors outside your control coming into a perfect constellation) is for those who aren't dedicated to having an elevated sex life. That's child's play. Instead, no matter how you feel or how dire the chasm is between you, if you're both all in, and want the life waiting for you on the other side, saying yes to sex is a key factor in getting you there.

We should note that during this process, you might need additional outside support to better understand what comes up for you. If this feels like you, then take action and get that support with a trained professional. You can visit laceyandflynn.com to learn more, or go out on your own and find a local practitioner who specialises in embodied coaching or a trauma-informed therapist.

Resistance

You know that feeling when you have to do something but you don't want to, and so your mind gets to work creating every excuse in the book to try and get out of it? Yup, that's resistance. Resistance is basically a refusal to accept or go along with something. Sure, we can be resistant to things for a good reason – perhaps they're not aligned or right for us – but for this exploration, this is resistance to things we want and *are* right for us, but that we can't bring ourselves to do. We see this resistance as both hands, energetically speaking, attempting to deflect, block and avoid something with all one's inner might. The resistance we're speaking about here is usually a solitary inner game to begin with. It happens in our minds as a series of excuses to block the potential for intimacy and sex.

Now why, when sex is meant to be such a wonderful, pleasurable experience, would resistance even factor in when the chance for lovemaking is on the table?

There's a cute wordplay around intimacy. It goes: 'into-me-I-see'. Intimacy, the energetic space of proximity, connection, familiarity and desire, isn't always a simple and easy one to navigate. If you're feeling any sort of sexual disconnect or emotional numbness, as if you're living a life that's not quite aligned or you're feeling lost to yourself, then intimacy, which could actually be the antidote, often feels, well – too intimate.

True intimacy means we have to shed the hard outer layer we've grown, let go and become soft and vulnerable like a turtle with no shell (but unlike a turtle with no shell, you're not going to die from this). For many, this vulnerability can be scary as hell. We don't want to look into ourselves or be seen fully, because, even if unintentionally, we've been avoiding this exact experience: slowing down enough to finally get present and real to who we are and how we're feeling in our lives.

Men are often much better at getting intimate without being intimate. They're able to engage in sex without emotional or spiritual proximity. Women tend to find this more challenging. And so, when the prospect of intimacy is on the table but the woman can sense there's no real intimacy to be had, or she isn't in a space to actually show up and reveal the depths of her heart and soul without it being reciprocated, it's easier to resist the situation.

For men, resistance doesn't tend to show up as a downright refusal to have sex or be together; instead, it shows up more as a block against truly opening up and being vulnerable. They're game for getting it on, but they'll do the dance of resistance around truly sharing and showing up from a place of full inner-self-revelation, because that space is so unfamiliar to them. They've had no model for deep sharing, nor experience in putting language to what they're feeling.

Resisting intimacy

This same resistance shows up when it comes to self-pleasure, and it shows up in the same way again for both men and women. Men will be happy to rub one out and achieve orgasm (masturbation), but actually dropping in, connecting with themselves on a more emotional and soulful level, and really feeling their bodies, might pose a significant challenge. This is terrain they haven't been used to navigating: being truly intimate with themselves. Men have often been encouraged to stay cool and detached, to not be overly emotional, available or vulnerable. But what we're asking men to do here is the exact opposite. In order to move into an elevated sex life, this often underdeveloped aspect of the masculine – being connected and intimate – needs to be seen and tended to (see pages 199–200, where we teach you everything about self-pleasure for men).

When it comes to women exploring self-pleasure, their resistance again will be present from the outset with nearly a downright refusal to show up and do the deed to begin with. There will be high levels of shame and a fear around getting caught or being found out. Pair that with the friction of actually slowing down, dropping in and being in a pleasure-state, it's easier to avoid, resist and find something that can actually be ticked off the to-do list to do (we get into this in full in chapter six, so hang tight).

Once a couple decides to begin this elevated sex journey in earnest, they'll also face the resistance of not wanting to do the very thing they've committed to doing: showing up for sex and intimacy, no matter the weather. This resistance is usually what derails the process entirely and, in our experience, personally and professionally, is often the hardest thing to navigate.

Resistance is tricky. It's tricky insofar as that it actually tricks us into believing we're not experiencing resistance, and instead have a really good reason for not wanting to do A, B or C. It's the number-one sticking point for most couples when they engage in this work, and we want to make sure you fully understand you're not alone in this – and that it is, in fact, surmountable.

For some, resistance will be cropping up again and again as you read every word on these pages. An indignant voice inside you will reject what it is you're reading. You'll push against the assertions we're making, you'll deny they have anything to do with you, and you'll even find yourself having an inner battle to stand up for your unique blend of resistance. 'I don't have resistance,' you'll say, 'it's just that all my partners haven't been open.' Or you'll say, 'I don't have resistance, I'm just busy and have enough on my plate without all this sex stuff to deal with.' Trust us: you're not alone in this inner pursuit to protect yourself from vulnerability, looking within and, ultimately, creating change.

From the outset, it would seem men, who are often more encouraging and vested in creating opportunities for sex in the relationship, would be more game to do this work, but the vulnerability aspect and showing up emotionally can pose enough of a challenge so as to fully derail the work before it even begins. Whereas a woman's resistance arises in a different way. She'll often be game to do the work from the outset, but when in practice, when it comes to actually doing the work (getting naked, having sex, sharing her body and being intimate), her resistance will rear its very irritable head and make it challenging for her to move beyond the talk-space, where she's sufficiently comfortable and would happily stay for the rest of her days. The fear for both here is moving from a known/safe space into the realm of exposing oneself through change.

What we want you to do is harness those sex-detective skills we mentioned earlier on to become very clear about when and where your resistance arises, and to resist falling prey to its very insistent and convincing pursuit of keeping you from healing and rising in your sexual expression. It's strange, isn't it? You're here wanting to create a thriving sex life, you know that sex is an extraordinary part of your existence as a human, you have an inner knowing of what could be possible for you if you up-levelled your sex life, and yet there's this very real part of you that wants to undermine the whole expedition.

And perhaps you've experienced this before across different facets of life with other things that matter to you. Maybe you've wanted to make a big change in your life, like changing careers or moving countries. Or perhaps there's been a conversation you've wanted to have with someone important, and you knew it needed to happen, but somehow you resisted. Resistance can be a protective mechanism wanting to keep us from being exposed, from potentially taking a step, missing and failing. Ultimately, it wants to keep us from rising out of what's comfortable and into the great unknowns of life.

What you need to remember, though, is that this aspect of the self isn't the truest self. It's simply a part of your inner workings, and it's not a part you need to spend time developing further. In fact, it's time to begin dismantling this aspect of yourself and seeing it for what it is: a limiter that's holding you back from growth, expansion, expression and, ultimately, for all intents and purposes, from sexual bliss. In learning to heal resistance, you'll not only mature as a sexually expressed human here to create a life of pleasure and exceptional orgasmic bliss, you'll also become a person who understands themselves better across all facets of life.

Because if resistance is messing with you in the bedroom, it's also going to be messing with you in the boardroom. When you become masterful at navigating the inner parts of you that are resisting vulnerability, closeness and self-expression, you win in all areas of your life, not just in your sexual relationship with yourself or someone else. You become someone who knows themselves, someone who doesn't fall prey to derailing themselves and staying small. You become a person who can see the difference between the highest expression of yourself and a small inner voice that can be very loud in its desire to keep you from reaching too far and perhaps missing in your pursuit of greatness, sexually and otherwise.

As a sexual detective, you're going to develop a spaciousness within, where you can pause at the gates of resistance and ask yourself: Why am I holding back? Is there something else going on here, besides what this inner voice is telling me? What's below my initial reaction and response? In asking yourself these questions and being fully open to receiving what wants to be revealed, you're going to stop getting blocked at the initial reactionary phase and begin moving and healing into the more substantial depths of who you are. It's very exciting stuff.

For years – literal years – Lacey's resistance was the most powerful derailing force in her life. And before she got on top of it and fully understood it, it was convincing and fully in charge.

6

LACEY

Even though I'd fully committed to healing our sex life and I'd made the commitment to myself and to Flynn, I was still battling with my small inner-self, which wanted to keep me from showing up and baring my soul. We'd have sex scheduled and days before the moment arrived I'd begin the dance of resistance, negotiating with myself, trying to plan my escape, coming up with every excuse in the book to avoid intimacy and connection. I was so afraid of slowing down, of showing up and dropping into this space of sexual discovery, that my small inner voice told me it would be better to accidentally fall off my bike or get stuck on the underground than actually show up for sex and intimacy.

FLYNN

There were definitely times where I had resistance to showing up for sex when we began this journey, because I knew I would have to be there for Lacey and support her emotionally so she would be able to meet me physically and, in turn, help me access a deeper emotional space within myself. Sometimes I resisted it because it was deep work and I simply didn't feel up to it. But ultimately, each time, I made the choice to show up, because I could see that sexy light at the end of the tunnel was worth reaching for.

9

Even now, years into this work in both our professional and personal lives, resistance is something we both navigate and face. The difference now, though, is that we can see it for what it is. It doesn't derail us; instead it is simply a part of the self that we can witness, identify and allow to exist without charging after it, amplifying it and listening to its persuasive ways.

How to face resistance

Recognise that you have it It's easy to shrug it off and say 'not me', but if you let your guard drop and admit there's some level of resistance, it will be infinitely easier to take the next steps on your journey.

Go easy Once you claim it, sit with it. It takes time to come to terms with all the ways in which we've held back from sex, intimacy and connection. There's no need to rush on the path of sexual healing and liberation.

Stretch gently into discomfort When you step outside your comfort zone, you grow. But you don't need to jump in the deep end if you haven't learned to swim. Yes, challenge yourself, but do it with care.

Understand the intricacies and resistance Look at all the ways resisting sex, intimacy or sexual connection has impacted not only your life between the sheets, but all other parts of your life, too.

> **Take action** Decide to do at least one practice from this book (self-pleasure, writing your sexual storyline, etc.) to get the energy moving in your life.

The Rejection Loop

LACEY

Flynn wasn't an easy-to-reject guy in the beginning. Rejecting him was a muscle I had to hone. It took repetition to be able to reject him easily – swiftly, even. And it took myriad excuses, which I would call on without even considering which one I was using, so that no matter what, I wouldn't have to have sex. It sounds callous, but rejecting his advances wasn't intentional. It was a reflex of trauma, a survival mechanism. I didn't know how to cope with sex and intimacy, and so avoiding it at all costs was all I knew how to do. At the time, I would never have described the situation as 'rejection'. I was convinced that my excuses were the real reason I didn't want to have sex. I was either too tired, or busy, or he'd done something to irk me – there were any number of reasons why it was easier to not have sex than it was to have it. I didn't realise then that we were in the Rejection Loop, and that rejecting him and his desire for sex had become my normal. It's important to note that deep down, I wasn't rejecting *him*. Even though it felt personal, it wasn't. I was rejecting myself, my pleasure and intimacy of any kind. I was rejecting getting close, being fully seen, letting go and opening up.

FLYNN

I always wanted Lacey to be happy, and at the same time to have my needs met. I wondered why we couldn't have both. At the beginning, I was okay to skip sex every now and then. After all, why would I want to have sex if Lacey didn't? But after some time, it began to mean that sex became more and more elusive. It's fascinating to think back and relive how painful and out of alignment this was for me. I didn't know how to express what I was feeling in a way that Lacey would be able to deeply understand. For her, it was all about her side of things, and much less about mine, because all she could see was the insurmountable irritation that she felt every time I made an advance. But from my side, I couldn't stop. It was too important to me.

———————————————— 𝟿 ————————————————

The Rejection Loop is what happens when a desire divide is born – one partner wants it more than the other, and the tactic for avoiding sex is that the person who doesn't want it rejects the person who does. This isn't something that happens once or twice; instead, this is an ongoing dynamic that plays out in the relationship, negatively impacting both people. It begins as the chemistry of the honeymoon phase wears off, attraction dwindles and the concept of not having sex becomes more enticing to one person.

One of the many painful attributes of the Rejection Loop is the way in which it emasculates a man and hardens a woman. In our personal and professional experience, it's usually the woman rejecting the man. Of course, there are other configurations of this that you might be experiencing, and all of them are valid. As always, we speak from our own experience, which is how we stay authentic and ultimately help others.

In the beginning, during the transition out of the honeymoon phase, we didn't know we were entering into the expanse we'd eventually dub the Rejection Loop. It just seemed like the normal trajectory to us: the hot and heavy period wanes, and in its place comes the part of the relationship where the guy wants it more than the woman, and she now has to spend her time deflecting his advances ad nauseam.

6

FLYNN

Naming and finally understanding this period in our relationship was eye-opening and healing for us both. I'd become this puppy, pawing at Lacey for years, just trying to connect, trying to get some intimacy. The more she rejected me, the more emasculated I felt – and, ultimately, the less attractive I was to her. What attracted her to me in the first place had been heavily eroded by my feeling so rejected. I wasn't able to show up as the man I wanted to be, as the man I ultimately was.

9

'Before we started learning about the Rejection Loop, arguments and perceived "rejection" during intimacy created a big void in the relationship and took us a few days to navigate. The key to us overcoming this has been focusing on practices that bring us into heart connection every day. Now the waves are simply breathed through and don't hold a charged impact.'

Emily (30) and Anton (29)

Usually what happens in this masculine-feminine dynamic is that the sex hasn't evolved in the relationship to be of full service to either person. Because the feminine requires a level of soulful, heart connection in order to fully expand into sexual expression, the sex becomes less interesting and enjoyable, because neither party knows how to make that happen.

Healing the Rejection Loop

The first step in healing this pattern is awareness and recognition that it's playing out. You can't actively heal what you don't see and recognise as problematic, so letting yourself see it for what it is and jointly naming it – the Rejection Loop – is the first step in mending this painful situation.

Changing the behaviour circuit doesn't happen overnight, and both partners will have work to do around this. The rejecting partner will have the task of unpacking the deeper reasons behind the excuses that have led to this level of rejection.

For the partner who is doing the rejecting, ask yourself:

- How long has the Rejection Loop been going on?
- Have you been in this same role before in a different relationship?
- How do you feel in your body when you reject your partner's advances?
- What is it you're afraid of when it comes to sex and intimacy?
- What would happen if you started to change your pattern and not reject your partner?
- Could you find a middle ground on the road to recovery?

Reflecting on these questions and getting honest with yourself before discussing it with your partner will give you a level of clarity and self-knowledge that will help you to more easily share and give insight into your side of the experience.

For the partner who is being rejected, ask yourself:

- How long have you been experiencing rejection of your sexual advances?
- How have you handled the rejection and how has it impacted you?
- What have you done with the insight your partner has shared with you around why they don't want to have sex?
- What do you need to do for yourself and the partnership to heal from the Rejection Loop?
- Consider what it would be like if it was all because of your actions and the way you had been showing up. What would you change?

For the rejected partner, getting clear on the ramifications of this level of rejection on your psyche and taking responsibility for your part of the dynamic is imperative. It's easy to dump the responsibility on the rejecting partner, as it might feel like the situation is entirely because of them, but each partner has played a part and it's important to understand the nuances of your position in this dynamic.

Alongside scheduling sex and showing up for sex as a practice (which we'll explore in chapter ten), healing the Rejection Loop will require a willingness to face resistance and shame, a commitment to tirelessly bridging the chasm, and a dedication to strengthening the opposite of rejection:

acceptance and receptivity. Where the energy was once one of closing down and saying no, the dynamic is going to shift to staying open and saying yes – yes to intimacy, connection, love, sex, togetherness and all the awkwardness and discomfort that comes when two people decide to face their sexual selves and their joint sexual dynamic, and move towards a thriving and elevated sex life.

Both partners will need to take full responsibility for themselves and move beyond blame into radical self-responsibility. Where once you wanted to be right and have your position heard, now the desire is to be curious and open. You must resist the urge to close down or shut up the expanse of your heart with the pettiness of trying to be right, and you must resist usurping the scenario by centring yourself instead of the joint mission of intimacy and love. To do this, patience with yourself and your partner is key. Listen to your body and your partner's, listen to one another's words, and be extremely curious about your own habitual tendencies. Take time to sit with everything, and use journaling as a tool for reflection while challenging what you believe to be true or 'the way it is' in favour of opening up to a new way of connecting and being in your relationship that is of deeper service to you both. This will be of benefit as you begin to visualise how things could be and work towards that, either together or solo.

On consent and how it works

In the beginning, as you work to mend the Rejection Loop, you'll take 'no' off the table completely. 'No' has been the go-to, and now it needs to be dissolved. There needs to be a new trust and vocabulary in order for progress to be made. It's time for 'yes' or 'yes and ...' instead of 'no' and 'but'.

Instead of saying no, you could say:

Partner A: I'd like to connect with you sexually now.

Partner B: Yes, I'm open to that, and I'd like to start really slowly, without expectation on an end goal or result.

This scenario takes the place of:

Partner A: I'd like to connect with you sexually now.

Partner B: No, I don't feel like it. I'm not in the mood.

Another example is this:

Partner A: Let's have sex!

Partner B: I have a lot of resistance and I want to show up and explore it together.

Instead of:

Partner A: Let's have sex!

Partner B: I'm tired, it's been a big day and I just want to watch TV.

We know taking 'no' off the table might feel dramatic, but we bet the above examples will help to lessen the blow. Of course, this doesn't mean you have to be having penetrative sex, riding cowgirl, or getting your balls licked twenty-four-seven. What it does mean is that intimacy and connection will now be on the table.

You might be asking yourself, 'Isn't everyone entitled to say "no", especially when it comes to sex and consent?' But this isn't about consent as we know it. This is a completely different lane on the journey of sex and intimacy.

A deep and personal consenting to the process must be granted in advance of doing this work – individually and as a couple – and this consent stands as a personal devotion to the process that usurps any moment-to-moment consenting practice. Of course, you never have to do anything you don't want to do, but by learning to say yes, you begin to tap in to your deeper self – the part of you that wants connection – instead of the triggered or reactionary self – the part of you that wants to run. If this isn't understood and practised by both partners, then you're probably not ready for this work. This journey is about both partners having equal power, equal commitment, equal responsibility and an equally strong 'yes' to the process and journey.

This might go without saying but we'll say it loud for everyone in the back: neither party, in integrity, can use this level of consent to manipulate the other person or the situation. If this is the intention, then again, this work is not appropriate for this relationship.

Only two fully consenting adults who are dedicated to their own spiritual, emotional and sexual expansion can undertake this work. Of course, we're all human, and there will be times when our own baggage, fear and projections get in the way of healing, but to be on this path, one must be dedicated to taking responsibility and ownership over one's reactions and ways of being in the world. This requires a level of self-attunement that most will never aspire to, let alone master. This is the way of the awakened being: desiring to do one's best on a soul level, committing to being in alignment with one's highest self, and sharing this with the person you're choosing to share your sexual expression with.

Trauma

Okay, we admit it – this section is huge and a bit on the heavy side. We're giving you a lot of dense matter, but it's not to depress you or overwhelm you, or make you think all hope is lost, relationships are shit and what's the point anyway?! We're top-loading the challenges in this book so that right from the get-go, you have all the potential issues you're coming up against laid bare, fully revealed and articulated. This shows you that a) we get it, b) you're not alone and c) nothing is left unsaid. So, in the name of getting it all out in the open, we're going to charge ahead with laying all this big stuff on the table so it's not hiding in the corners holding any cards.

Trauma informs the trajectory of our lives. There's no secret there. Sure, there's the immediate physical impact of something horrible happening, but what we're exploring here are the long-term ramifications of an incident that occurred where the person wasn't able to process, deal with or express their experience or the emotional impact. We're not professionals in the field of trauma, but we have worked with countless individuals who are mending from past circumstances – some horrendous, some relatively mild – that have an impact on their present reality. When it comes to sex and intimacy, it's impossible to do this work without addressing trauma. We encourage you to take action and find someone who specialises in the field of trauma to support you if trauma is seriously blocking you from living life to the fullest.

Lacey worked through quite a bit of her own trauma directly through sex. This method will not be for everyone, nor do we recommend it or advise it to anyone. On that note, since we don't know you, we don't recommend or advise anything to you specifically. As we explained at the start, if you're going to do this work, you're going to have to create your own protocol and network of support, and be responsible for yourself. The truth is, we're all moving about the world with trauma, because we've all experienced wounding that's not been tended to, healed and loved in order to integrate into the whole of our being. And many people have experienced trespassing on their bodies – negative sexual experiences – or have witnessed such things in the lives of others.

Trauma will impact your rate of healing and your overall capacity for digging in and doing this work. There's nothing wrong with that. What we do know is that this work should not be the first port of call, especially if something sexually, physically or emotionally traumatising has happened in your life. This work is usually best done after you've worked one-on-one with a professional or explored in-person modalities that have supported you and brought you further along the path.

Triggers

You might notice throughout this work that you become triggered: that you shut down, flare up or have an embodied or
emotional response that's powerful and perhaps unpleasant.
It's not uncommon for this to happen. As you get to know
yourself more fully, and as you heal, you'll probably begin
to feel or experience things that have been pressed into the
corners of your being. For example, if something happened
in the past when you were giving oral sex that felt humiliating,
you might experience that humiliation again while giving
oral sex, even if this current situation is safe and positive. Our
bodies remember and our psyche holds what we were previously unable to articulate or process.

Depending on the severity of the experience and your own
skills and knowledge of self-holding, you might be able to
navigate this and, in time, reprogramme your response.
Alternatively, it might be too much, and you may have to
stop, pause and breathe to find your centre again. This
can be scary and destabilising. In the pages that follow,
we'll give you tools for unpacking, understanding and navigating these experiences. Know you're not alone and be
tender with yourself, always pressing gently into discomfort
but never throwing yourself over the edge prematurely. To
have progress you need to be with what is, and that can
take time to unfold.

Voicing the unspoken

We're laying out some big challenges that exist when it
comes to sex and intimacy in general (solo or partnered),

as well as sex in long-term relationships. In going no holds barred into the shadows and grit, we hope to illuminate all the things you might be encountering and give voice to these often unspoken experiences. We've found that for many, it's not just that these experiences are unspoken, they're also not recognised or witnessed.

Awareness is the first step in healing. We have to become aware that there's an issue, and we have to become well versed in what this issue is if we're to comprehend the ramifications and ultimately move in the direction we truly want for ourselves, our partnerships and our lives as a whole.

We don't view what we're sharing as dire or awful in the least. Even though the stuff of this section is heavy, it actually excites us and makes us feel light to be sharing it with you. That's because we've been through it, and have coached and taught countless others who have as well. Instead of this being a big downer, we're thrilled to be giving a voice to what we see as an area of life and partnerships that has been grossly underrepresented, and thus has wreaked monumental havoc for individuals and relationships. We don't want any more relationships to be doomed from the outset because people are underequipped to deal with their own relationships to sex and how to navigate intimacy in the long run. We don't want an epidemic of low-vibe lovers who scarcely know what it is to love, and are more prone to walking away than turning in to the challenges and potential for growth that relationships offer.

Exploring trauma

Here are a series of questions to ask yourself to help you understand if a past situation or experience is currently adversely impacting your ability to connect sexually, to yourself or someone else.

Ask yourself:

- Is a past sexual experience currently impacting my ability to be intimate?
- Have I done anything so far to explore, understand and heal this trauma?
- Am I ready to work more deeply to unpack the impact of this experience?
- What do I need to feel safe and supported on this journey?
- Is there anyone in my life with whom I can share this so I feel less alone?
- How can I hold myself with love and care so that I can begin to heal and thrive as a sexually expressed person?

Please note, the answers to these questions will change as you venture further down your path. We often advise students who are at a place where they're ready to work on a body level to begin with self-pleasure. This doesn't need to elicit pleasure to begin with. It can simply be self-touch, exploring the body and taking note of what happens. More will be taught on self-pleasure and self-connection practices to promote self-love and healing in chapter six.

We feel relationships are sacred lands, ripe with potential for ascension, grounding, growth and self-realisation. In some ways, even though we have sex on our podcast and talk about some pretty out-there things, we're old-fashioned in our belief that monogamy and long-term relationships hold unparalleled power and can be portals to transformation, not only on the family level but also on the community and global levels.

With that boost of inspiration and go-get-'em tiger energy, let's circle back around and finish up this section on all the monumental challenges that arise when it comes to navigating sex and intimacy, with yourself and someone else, by talking about shame.

Shame

Shame is a very real beast. It comes dark, dreary and heavy, weighing us down and highlighting all the ways in which we're yucky, unworthy and awful beings. Shame will draw us away from connection, both to ourselves and to others, and into a place where self-loathing and personal belittlement take centre stage. When it comes to sex, shame can be the quicksand that keeps you from fully expressing, understanding or sharing yourself. Shame is defined as that painful and icky feeling inside when you're humiliated, when you feel like you've done something wrong or somehow acted foolishly.

To get to the core of it – because shame is a huge terrain when it comes to sex – let's take some time to break down common ways in which shame might rear its ugly energy and derail you from full sexual liberation.

Self-pleasure and shame

Let's start at the start. When you were young, you may have been taught that touching yourself was dirty and wrong. From your early beginnings, you learned that even though it felt good, it wasn't right and that engaging in self-touch was bad behaviour, and maybe even made you a bad person. Imagine the impacts of this programming. Your body, your precious little body, craving exploration and the excitement of self-induced pleasure, was made wrong. You were made wrong, the pleasure was made wrong, and so your relationship to this very important and powerful part of your sexual expression was riddled with shame from the start.

You might not have had such a dire experience with being shamed around self-pleasure, but we're sure you've encountered various shades of shame, or heard embarrassing stories, when it came to your body or the bodies of others, masturbation or even having sexual desire to begin with. This is such a prevalent experience that we're willing to wager every person who reads this book has, at some point, experienced shame around touching themselves, which of course carries over into adult life, influencing sexual relationships and one's own connection to pleasure.

The first step is to recognise, with so much kindness for yourself, that you have shame around touching your own body. The second step is not to go wild and just start shaking hands with Mr Winky or dialling the rotary phone; it's to acknowledge the impacts of this shame. Sometimes we want to act casual, like it's no big deal, when in actuality, this shame has probably left you feeling scared, on edge or gross about your own body's desires. Get real with yourself by having a solid think about it, and then make sure to do the tasks in chapter four around unpacking your sexual storyline.

Shame and communication

Now imagine having your first experiences of sexual expression riddled with shame. What are the implications of this on your ability to discuss sex and intimacy with friends, parents or a lover? Most adults lack the language for discussing sex and intimacy (we'll get to this in chapter five, where we dive into everything involving communication, including power language and using your voice to share your inner world).

We don't have words that make us feel good when discussing our bodies and our experiences, and we feel the utmost shame in simply addressing sex. Something we've heard from new students more than a handful of times is that just by discussing signing up to work with us – in our online course Sex Elevated, for instance – couples of many years, sometimes decades, spoke more about sex and intimacy than they ever had before.

For most, even if there are glaring issues, conversations around sex and intimacy will be avoided at all costs. There's so much uncertainty: a fear of being wrong or seeming foolish, not wanting to rock the boat or make your partner feel bad. Instead, couples will live for years in dissatisfaction, with petty resentments cropping up and small irritations turning into mountains, before they actually sit down and talk about what's truly happening. And this is because people are ill-equipped to take responsibility for themselves, to show up and communicate powerfully and with integrity, around a matter that's very sensitive.

We're delighted to be giving you the tools here to do this work, not only for yourself and your relationship, but for the world at large. More mature, self-reflective and fully self-responsible beings who can talk about sex and intimacy and the big challenges of communicating and relating will do nothing but great things for the overall fabric of society.

The first step is to have a conversation with the old numero uno: you. Get real with yourself on the calibre of your communication when it comes to sex and intimacy.

- Do you have a tendency to share openly or hide your feelings and desires?
- What have been the ramifications of not speaking your sexual truth?
- How would your life feel different if you felt safe to speak openly about sex?

Shame and your body

Let's get honest here about the level of shame you carry around your body. Never mind your sexual body for a moment; simply think about your body as a whole. Consider the shame you have around your size, weight, hair (or lack thereof), the way you look naked, your skin, your smell – chances are, you've judged every part of yourself with a harsh word and gaze many times over in your life, possibly many times over every day.

Now, let's throw your sexual body into the mix – your boobs, nipples, bum, cock, balls, vulva – what awful things have you felt, said and believed to be true about these precious and extraordinary parts of your being? Then, on top of this layer of judgement, add in the mega shame that people don't even recognise they have just for being a sexual being with body parts attributed to sex and sexual expression. It's like just the act of being and having a body is enough to elicit shame.

If you're reading this and thinking, *That's not me*, humour us for a moment and pause to reflect on the shadowy and slithery underbelly of shame that might not be at the surface of your awareness, but exists as an undercurrent, undermining your relationship to your body and sex. Again, wagers on the table and all chips in, we're willing to bet every single set of eyes reading these words is connected to a dear human who has felt shame around their sexual bodies. How then, with this level of unchecked, repressed and unhealed shame, could anyone be expected to thrive in a sexual relationship?! How can an elevated sex life even be possible if you're scarcely willing to look at, witness, let alone love your own body or let someone else fully adore you?

Often, we don't recognise how our relationships to our bodies stunt our ability to thrive in a sexual relationship. Because sexual expression and intimacy are expressions of the body, it follows that your relationship to your body – and often this is more about your *perception* than the actual fabric of your body – will impact your experience of sex. If you feel ashamed of your body, if you feel like your body is wrong simply for being, it's going to be hard to fully show up, be vulnerable and allow yourself to express the full, raw desire of your sexual body, with yourself or with someone else. We'll get into this fully in chapter six, and share insight into healing this, but for now, this is about becoming aware and clear on what might be happening so we can eventually take the next step towards healing and elevating.

We're excited to take you on a journey of Cock- and Pussy Gazing in chapter six, which will blow your mind (and eyes) as you see yourself anew – and perhaps for the very first time. For now, start your body-healing journey by acknowledging there might be shame that needs exploring. Let yourself feel into the impacts that this shame has had on your life as a whole and your ability to connect intimately with yourself or someone else.

A few questions to ask yourself:

- Do you feel ashamed about any parts of your body?
- When you think about the past, do you carry shame with you about any previous sexual experiences?
- As it stands now, what is the impact of shame on your current experience of sex or your sexual journey to date?

Shame and being seen

Our last stop on the shame circuit is a little place we call 'Being Seen'. To achieve the vulnerability and openness necessary to create a truly thriving sexual dynamic requires letting yourself see and be seen at depths and heights perhaps never previously explored.

You think: What happens if I look foolish? What happens if I show too much of myself, let go, get wild and can't take it back? What happens if I tell the truth about what I like and what I want, and I'm rejected?

It's scary territory, to open up and let yourself truly be you. We can often avoid it, not intentionally, but just as part of the natural journey of getting acquainted. In the early stages of a relationship, because we're getting to know one another, even the stuff on the surface can appear to have depth because we're seeing it for the first time. We're caught up in the lustre of lust and longing, and usually at this stage, we aren't getting to know the intricacies of the other person. We put our best foot forward and keep under wraps the more raw, unpolished bits that are scary to reveal because they're not performative – they're true. And when there's truth, we can vacillate between having confidence in our truth, and feeling tender and afraid to expose the soft underbelly of our being. But you deserve to see and be seen. The wholeness of who we are is not to be hidden, and is crucial to deep, meaningful, elevated sex.

The next time you have sex, try telling your partner exactly what it is you want and then notice how it feels to state this out loud. You can even start by telling the person you're with that you'd like to play a game where you both take turns expressing your desires. To elevate the experience further, make sure to share how you feel after you've stated your desires. If you feel vulnerable or silly, say it. If it feels hot and dirty, proclaim it. It's important to bookend the vulnerability of professing your desires by stating the impact sharing has had on you, so you acknowledge and understand your own feelings in the moment.

Ego and setting aside the small self

When you're on the path of elevated sex and creating a thriving sex life where both partners want it, you'll have to learn the art of setting aside your 'small self', healing ego-driven tendencies, and fully showing up in order to grow, mature and understand yourselves and one another more fully. When you get stuck in your small self, wanting to be right or wanting to protect yourself from getting it wrong or taking missteps, the depth of intention – to heal, change, elevate and grow – gets swept to the side in order to preserve the ego of one instead of the integrity and expansion of both.

What is the small self?

This is the part of you that's driven by ego, afraid to be wrong or foolish; the part that wants to stick with what's comfortable and easy. It's not a part of you that requires condemnation. Instead, witnessing and understanding this aspect of you is imperative on the journey towards elevated sex.

The small self . . .

- is the part of you that wants to be right
- is afraid of making mistakes or getting things wrong
- is happy staying small and not rocking the boat
- protects you from growth and change at all costs
- projects on to others instead of taking responsibility
- is reactionary instead of reflective

It's time to explore how you can learn and grow, not how you can always be right. Learning not to take it all so personally is a huge task of the sexual explorer. Sure, this is easier said than done. What else is more personal than getting naked, being intimate and sharing the fullness of your body, desire and pleasure with another human? Sex is personal because of the proximity, the tenderness, the intimacy of it all. But what doesn't need to be personal are the growing pains on the journey towards creating a thriving sex life.

For example, say one person doesn't like something: a certain kind of touch, or a certain position. They summon the courage to share this preference with the other partner. The small self will take this personally, and instead of hearing their partner say, 'I don't like this touch or position,' they'll hear, 'I don't like it *when you do* X, Y, Z.' Instead of hearing the experience of the other, we hear how *we* did something wrong and make it about ourselves instead of about the desires of the other person. In that moment, which could be about celebrating the partner who had the courage the share their truth, we take it personally; we make it about ourselves and lose the chance for immediate change, growth and a deepening of trust and of the relationship.

This is what we mean by setting aside the small self, and listening and attuning from the soul self instead of the ego-driven self. The ego self is all about self-preservation, being right, never being embarrassed and, ultimately, staying as far away from vulnerability and radical self-responsibility as possible. By contrast, the soul self – or the sexual soul self – is all about curiosity and not going with the immediate impulse to be right.

This higher self doesn't care for deflecting blame, and doesn't even factor blame into the equation to begin with, because it doesn't care for being right. Instead, what it values most is joy, happiness, connection and love. If this part of you is attuned to on the regular, it becomes stronger and a more dominant aspect of your personality. The small-ness you once felt at making everything personal subsides in favour of seeing more clearly, being less hot-headed or emotionally swept up, and becoming more grounded in your centre as a maturing person who prioritises con-nection over being right. This is a helluva great way to be, as a human in the world and as a partner in a thriving relationship.

Sex doesn't have a problem

We've introduced you to a wide array of factors that con-tribute to sexual challenges in the depths of long-term relationships. If you didn't feel seen and understood in what you've experienced in your life before this moment, or what you have witnessed in others, we hope that this part of the *Come Together* journey gave you some insight, and offered you the relief of finally having words for and clarity around some of the challenges that have cropped up on your path as a sexually expressive person.

Truth be told, though, there really isn't an issue with sex, is there? Sex doesn't have a problem. Sex shows us all the ways in which we're holding back, all the ways in which we've not learned about true love for self and other, and all the parts of ourselves that are ripe and ready to be healed so that we can live more connected, powerful and enjoyable lives.

Don't let your sexual challenges dissuade you from intimacy or a belief that epic, elevated sex is possible for you. Any challenge – whether born from trauma, dis-ease or disease, interpersonal challenges, shame or physiological issues – can be alleviated and expressed through the dance of sex. Of course, you might have things you need extra assistance with, but none of it is insurmountable. Your intention and desire for more can easily become more powerful than your history or the remnants of the past that still linger in your body, waiting to be felt, expressed, released and integrated.

We didn't know how we'd go from having what felt like insurmountable challenges in relating to having the best sex of our lives, but what we did know was that we felt an inner calling to explore and go deep to try and figure it all out.

Because, as we often both say after having sex, sex is the best! What's more fun than tapping into your body's infinite potential for pleasure? The answer is nothing. The kind of high and ecstasy available through sex is what many people confusedly spend their entire lives chasing through material gain and intoxicating substances. Sex is the ultimate high, it's the ultimate expression of creativity and love, and it's the best activity, physically and spiritually, you can do with yourself or with someone else.

It's easy to be scared of this level of self-expression. We haven't been taught how to let ourselves go, to drop into the depths of our bodies and to trust what spontaneously comes through as a result of being so present and so available to pleasure. In fact, pleasure has been demonised, corrupted and perverted in many ways. We've forgotten that pleasure isn't about gluttony or overindulgence or buying something; pleasure is an embodied experience that comes through activating the senses and being in integrity with what's truly good for you at all levels of your being.

Imagine the kind of life you'll live as a fully sexually expressed being, free of body shame and pleasure shame, capable of communicating your deepest desires, wants and needs, and able to hear another's truth without making it about you. What kind of world would it be if we all lived from that place of embodied power? Let's find out, shall we? Let's open up to the possibility of a world where people from all walks of life engage in embodied living where they prioritise their sexual joy, while being respectful and full of integrity towards both themselves and everyone with whom they exchange this energy.

Children would then grow up loving their bodies and feeling safe to express themselves. Relationships would be valued, with a reverence for partnerships, family and community as a whole. We're here for it. We're here for all of it. And we're cheering you on as you witness yourself more fully and take this next step on your elevated sex journey.

The issue with sex in long-term relationships, distilled

- Understand what's getting in the way of you and elevated sex.
- If there's trauma to unpack, do this in a way that's supported, with a trauma-informed practitioner who gets it.
- If you're in the Rejection Loop, facing resistance or in some way stuck when it comes to being intimate in a fulfilling and meaningful way, acknowledge it.
- Start getting clear on all the ways in which you're triggered when it comes to sex, intimacy and your body, so you can mend these and evolve beyond them.
- Give yourself full permission to go into the corners of your shame so you can stop being afraid to be wrong, both in your sexual expression and in life as a whole.
- Don't let your small self rule the show, or else you'll stay stuck in the land of mediocre boning.

3

Your new sex

Welcome to your new sex: an entirely new perspective on what sex could be. This is the moment when radical self-responsibility gets initiated and when each person claims their own turn-on, and stops passing the buck on their arousal (or lack thereof) on to their partner.

The new sex that we're teaching here is one of self-empowerment. One where each partner lives life from a lit-up place, where sexual energy is no longer relegated to the bedroom, and where couples integrate their desire into the totality of their lives.

We want everyone – singles and couples included – to move from pelvic-thrust sex to full-body, heart-engaged lovemaking. In this new space of sexual expression, emotions are tapped into and no longer turned away from, and couples are courageous and willing to show themselves in their full vulnerability as we shift from the age of greyscale intercourse to technicolour boning.

'The deep work I've done on understanding myself and my relationship with pleasure has had a profound impact on my life. I've learned that when I'm tired or can't be bothered, this often leads to the best sex! I actually need sex to keep me in my highest vibrational frequency, to then better serve my wife, family, work and wider community.'

Theo (27)

So, how do you get from run-of-the-mill shagging to this over-the-rainbow pleasure-fest we're talking about here? Glad you quietly wondered that to yourself. Let's dig in.

The pillars of elevated sex

We have a little acronym from our online course, Sex Elevated: SIRCH.

These are the pillars that we teach singles and couples to keep in mind, embody and implement when they begin the journey of relating sexually in this newfound way.

Here's a basic outline of how the pillars work in action:

Surrender

Let go of your expectation, release what you thought you knew, let go of what you want to happen, and open up to a totally new way of relating. Allow yourself to be present to the natural unfolding of the process. Turn away from expectation.

Intention

Bring conscious awareness into the mix and set an intention for why you're doing this work, what you want to feel and what's at the core of the journey for you.

Reframe

At every stage and in every way, take a fresh perspective. Reframe situations to see a new viewpoint, take things that once felt negative and remove the charge. Depersonalise the process and instead be a curious observer willing to explore every angle. Question your habits.

Communication

Let your heart, mouth, genitals and body talk. Elevate your language to Power Language (see pages 150–7), claim your voice and desires, and say the words you might never have said. Now is the time to speak your truth.

Hold space

Create a spacious and sacred container for this work. Hold the space for yourself and your own unfolding, and hold the space for the other person's experience. Take up space, and also learn to de-centralise yourself and let the other person take their space.

When summoned, these pillars tend to transform the sexual dynamic. People get out of their own way, and open to new possibilities beyond what they've experienced in the past. They begin the process of dissolving being goal-orientated in favour of journey-focused sexual expression, they become more aware of their own limiting beliefs and patterns, and they start taking radical self-responsibility instead of passing the buck to their partner.

Your turn-on belongs to you

What would it look like if you became entirely responsible for your own turn-on? Let us explain.

Instead of relying on someone else to arouse you, turn you on or get you in the mood, what would it look like if you took full ownership over this process and over your own sexual energy, and brought that to your lovemaking experience?

In action, this looks like being your own greatest lover, loving your body, and believing in the importance and power of being a sexually connected and liberated autonomous being. It's about arriving to sex with your sexual energy already activated, instead of it being dormant or relying on the other person to ignite it.

'After starting to process and integrate my childhood and early adulthood religious sexual repression, I was able to fully embrace my own pleasure in a way I hadn't been able to access before. Making space for and amplifying pleasure and joy, and allowing my turn-on to lead the way in my life, has been a game-changer. Our sex life is now light years more electrifying for both of us, and my husband is super turned on and inspired by my confidence, expressiveness and ability to vocalise desires.'

Aisha (32)

To go further, imagine this ...

You arrive to a sex session and you feel confident, clear and connected to yourself. Your body is alive with feeling. The numbness you once experienced with regard to sexuality or desire is gone, and in its place, you are deeply aware of and aligned with what you want and how to get what you want – not as an act of taking from the other, but as a self-anchored process of right communication, action and self-possession.

You're activated emotionally and physically. Your emotions – energy in motion – move through you easily, and you feel safe in yourself and able to express what you're experiencing. Your body, which once wasn't fully known by your own hands and heart, is now your dearest ally. You know your body, you've woken up your body, and you feel turned on – to life and lovers, and most importantly, to yourself.

Sounds pretty great, doesn't it?

Have you ever been in a sex session where you felt irked because the other person just didn't get it? They couldn't turn you on and you left feeling like there was simply something off with the dynamic, or something wrong with the other person.

This isn't about getting it on with someone you don't have any chemistry with or desire for. We don't want you to bypass attraction and alignment. Instead, we want you to understand the nuanced world of attraction, and to no longer defer your power based on someone else's level of hotness, ability or presence.

Sure, you want to be showing up for someone who is also showing up for themselves. It's definitely not an easy path to be awakening sexually alongside a partner who's not committed to doing the same level of work.

Let's look at it this way . . .

You're receiving oral sex. It's the start of the sex session, and you're wanting to get lit up and turned on. But it's not working. You're flaccid or dry, your mind is wandering and you're not even really connected into the feeling, because your thoughts are too loud, your body seems unreceptive, and now the sensations the other person is imparting on to you with their mouth are starting to be a bit bothersome. You want to enjoy it but you're not fully feeling it; they're not lighting you up, and it's all a bit annoying.

This scenario right here is a super-common one, and is often the result of deferred turn-on and living disconnected from sexual core energy.

What we see in this example is a lack of presence and connection to self, which is often a result of lifestyle, awareness and, ultimately, choices. We see a mind-body fracture, where the mind is rampant and the body dormant, and as a result, we get an inability to come online sexually, because the sexual flame hasn't been tended to in daily life. The body is probably experiencing numbness – not always on a tangible physiological level, but on a deeper level where energy and emotions create a divide within the experience. In the end, that chap, chappy or chapette lapping it up between your legs really doesn't stand a chance, because – let's face it – you can't get cum from a stone, can you?

And no, we're not suggesting you're a stone. You're a living, fleshy being, capable of full turn-on in and of yourself, with a staggering orgasmic potential that's probably just been untapped to date.

Turn yourself on

Lighting your own fire and being your own raging sex flame is the key to epic sex. This doesn't mean you become some narcissistic fiend pining after your own reflection. It means you turn to yourself first, fill your own cup, and share your sexual expression from a place of self-connection and self-love.

The turned-on woman

- Put on a song and dance with yourself, for yourself, letting the movement generate in your hips and pelvis. Imagine your pelvis is full of honey. Swirl it around your whole body and enjoy the journey of dropping inward.
- Dress sexy, but not in a performative way for someone else. Dress in a way that makes you feel like a sex-bomb goddess, your highest self.
- Don't be afraid to lie back and rest instead of continuing with your insurmountable to-do list. Your filled cup makes you delicious.

The turned-on man

- Throw some logs around, work out, get sweaty and connect to your body. Getting yourself fired up and in your body is a hot ticket towards lighting your own sexual flame.

- Put in effort so that when you look in the mirror, you feel proud and elevated. This doesn't mean adhering to stereotypes of manly perfection; it means expressing your highest self so you feel good about you.
- Stay motivated and in the centre of your life, instead of passive or apathetic. This energy is often key to male sexual satisfaction, helping you feel like the king that you are.

If you're sitting there thinking, 'This isn't me,' then maybe there are other ways you can relate to what we're saying.

Now is the moment to get curious and open up a little more.

Maybe you've been with someone who you haven't been able to turn on, and you felt inadequate for not delivering. Or perhaps you can relate on some level to the person who felt uninterested sexually and, no matter what, couldn't get 'in the mood'.

We'll talk more about the myth of 'the mood' in chapter ten, but for now, please know, the mood isn't real. We know, you might instantly feel inclined to reject this assertion. 'Of course the mood is real, or else how would I be up for sex?' you might be saying. What we've discovered though, is that, living a life reliant on the mood is a ridiculous approach to becoming empowered sexually. More on this later.

For now, back to your turn-on.

When you take responsibility for your own arousal, you become a lit-up person who tends to their own sexual flame. This can look like self-pleasure and self-touch, healing your storylines around sex (see chapter four), reclaiming ownership of your body, loving your body in all ways and ultimately being the captain of your own ship. When the person who knows you best, who has explored all the nooks and crannies, and who is healed/healing of shame and open to giving and receiving from a place of connection and power is you, then you're on your way to elevated sex.

We want you to challenge the status quo and open up to a new level of personal sexual ownership. Just imagine what your life and sex life would look like if you took this level of responsibility for yourself.

Why is sex so hard?

Without sex, there is no us. So why in the hell is it such a challenging topic? 'How come,' as a morning TV host asked us, 'we're getting it so wrong?'

There are loads of reasons why we've got it wrong, including religion, cultural stories and beliefs, upbringing, lifestyle, and confusion over who we are as a species and what we're capable of.

6

LACEY

I remember being in a university class. There was a discussion happening around humans and where we sat in reference to other beings. It was about sex and gender. I remember the lecturer saying something along the lines of, 'It's been a long time since we've been animals' – as if, at some point, we stopped being animals and became some other type of being altogether; a being that existed outside nature. I was appalled, actually. I argued vehemently for our rightful place in the natural order of this world. It seemed to me then that a lot of people had a different viewpoint, believing our species existed outside or above the rest of creation – based on our cognitive capacity, perhaps, or our impetus to dominate, which has positioned us outside nature, our place of origin and rightful home.

9

Believing we're outside of nature while being entirely made of it, driven by it and enlivened by it, has head-, heart- and soul-fucked us all in the worst possible way. We're a con-fused bunch, we humans, driven by constructs instead of an attunement to our truest nature. Yes, we've developed powerful minds, but have we done it at the cost of feeling in our bodies? Have we gone too far?

We feel ashamed when we feel like animals: when we grunt in guttural ways while fucking, when we shit and someone smells it, or when we eat big, drippy bites with reckless abandon. We've inflated our minds and belittled our bodies, believing that intellect reigns supreme over the corporeal, and so things to do with the body became taboo and uncomfortable. We've got it entirely wrong and we're misaligned because of it, living unfulfilling lives and upholding fractured relationships that aren't serving our basic animal needs of pleasure, embodiment, sexual expression, and living a body existence free of shame, self-doubt and all the dis-eases created by dissociating from our truest nature.

We know: it sounds dire. And you know what? It is.

Our rejection of our own nature means we've rejected the nature of our home, destroying it while we destroy our own precious human lives, prioritising dominance over harmony. We live and screw from our heads, with little regard for the interwoven qualities of all existence, of all beings, and for all sexual interactions that could be holy instead of transactional.

Obviously, we've struck a chord here, inside ourselves – and perhaps inside you, too.

You know that feeling like there's something more for you in this life? Like you didn't come here just to work hard and die? Like there's more to your relationship than watching TV every night for the next three decades, then watching one another wither and fade into oblivion?

You do not exist outside of nature, of creative expression, of sexual potency. You are that. It is you. There's a Sanskrit saying – a *Soham* – meaning 'I am that':

I am nature.

I am sex.

I am desire.

I am animal.

I am god or the divine or whatever word you use for the greatest expression of creative energy.

I am everything.

Now, with all that at heart, how does a being who embodies all of this beauty and power show up in the world? Like a motherfucking goddess or god, that's how.

You claim your turn-on – which, hopefully, you can now understand as being far more important than showing up for a quick orgasm. This is the expression of your life-force energy and now is the time to claim it, nurture it and express it for the full enjoyment of this here human life. Pretty cool, right?

Claiming your sexual desire

Because you've been disconnected from your truest sexual expression beyond performance, you've probably also been disconnected from your desires. Sure, you might know what you like on the surface and how to get off, but do you know the full range of your body? Do you know what lights you up, what you long for – and, most importantly – what you long for once you stop suppressing your primal desires?

In our experience, most people don't have a clue what they want – in life or in the bedroom. They have an automatic response that skims the surface, but underneath that, there's no nuance or intricacy to colour the landscape of desire and bring it to life.

It's not that it's not there. Desire is there for every single one of us. But for many, it's subterranean, having never been fully tapped, expressed or given a place.

You might have desires of which you're ashamed, desires that scare you; you might feel nothing, be desire-less, devoid of longing and hunger.

Desire, like most great things, has had a bad rap. It's been seen as wrong, sinful and associated with the perverted among us. Acting on your deepest desires can be distorted into being seen as selfish, unnecessary and probably shameful (whether those desires are sexual or the stuff of big, lifelong dreams).

One thing that must come alive in each and every one of us is a feeling of worthiness around asking for and receiving what we want, from life and love. If you don't feel worthy of your desires, then it will be hard to connect to them, to ask for them and to accept them if they materialise.

Something to understand about worth, though, is that it's inherent. We don't become worthy by doing; we are worthy by *being*. What you want, as long as it's aligned and in integrity, is meant for you. You are worthy of these things – and not because you've necessarily done something to deserve them. We don't have to do A to get B. Love is for us all; abundance is for us all; feeling free, happy and content is for us all.

These are not experiences for a chosen few, and the belief that they are is something we need to rectify in order to claim desire. Sometimes, you may feel like asking, 'Who am I to ask for so much?' In the bedroom, you might feel like it's asking too much to have a soulful lover. And in life, you might feel it's asking too much to have more than enough to get by. How you perceive your worth will define what you ask for and whether you get it.

This is a law of manifestation – the co-creation of your reality. If you don't truly feel deserving of what you ask for, if you don't believe it's possible for you and thus don't take big action in the direction of your desires, you won't get what you want. You'll work hard, with one foot on the gas and the other on the brake, holding yourself back from the greatness you desire.

Claiming your desire by embodying it is paramount.

Who do you become when you let yourself feel worthy of and then claim your deepest desires? You become a person who stands tall, centred in themselves, alive in this moment and holding a possibility mindset from which to view and experience life. In the bedroom, you become a confident lover, no longer guided by shame that you're somehow wrong, or fear of being rejected in your truth.

Listen: you might want to have a finger thrust in your ass during sex, and perhaps this makes you feel wrong, perverted and shameful. You might desire to give up your hard-earned career and live in a sleepy village next to the ocean, which confuses you and makes you scared, since what you want deep down seems to be in opposition to how you're living and what you've been taught is the 'right way'.

It's interesting, isn't it, that our desires often feel at odds with our reality. Why is that? Why is it that what you want challenges what you have and how you're already living? And how do you heal this and centre your desires for a fulfilling and lit-up life?

It all starts in the bedroom

If you can pinpoint your desires, claim them, vocalise them and fulfil them in the bedroom, then you can probably do this across every other avenue of life, too.

Someone who can unashamedly connect into and then live out their sexual desires – from a place of soul-attunement, so the body is satisfied and the soul is nourished – is a person who is probably living a freer and more expansive and expressive life.

So what's getting in the way of you knowing what you want and how to get it? How could your life transform if you boldly explored some of your desires?

Imagine you completely knew your greatest desires and you believed in your ability to make them manifest. Imagine there was no part of you that felt ashamed of what you wanted, or felt you needed to explain yourself or protect yourself from ridicule or judgement. Imagine your desire-space felt like a juicy playground where you connected into your wants with ease, and then acted on them (or let them unfold with grace).

Please note, it's important to differentiate a reckless impulse born of fracture or misalignment from a soul-centred urge. One probably isn't coming from a place of integrity, and perhaps is unsafe (emotionally, physically and spiritually), while the other is in service to self and others. This isn't about fulfilling a desire born of distortion and illusion. This is about fulfilling desire born of a deep, healthy and whole relationship to the self, aligned with the self.

If your desires are pure – even if they're wild and weird – nothing is wrong about that.

You want to eat pussy while having your nipples tweaked and your butt licked? Cool, why not?

You want to have group sex and suck three different cocks at once? Cool, why not?

You want to have your mouth finger-fucked while your earlobe gets nibbled? Cool, why not?

You see, none of these things is inherently wrong, gross or weird. It's just the storylines that might make them seem taboo, scandalous, sinful or shameful. None of these acts is inherently anything. They are simply actions carried out by bodies that are probably longing for a certain experience and kind of fulfilment. When put that way, it becomes quite uncomplicated, doesn't it?

But how do you get to place where you can claim desires that seem outrageous to you now?

The answer: start practising. First with yourself, then perhaps with someone else.

How to begin claiming your desires

Ask yourself:

- What do I want in sex?
- What do I want in life?
- What's one big desire I have that I've never admitted out loud, or don't believe is possible for me?

Grab a pen and write it down. Now, choose any one of the desires and ask yourself this:

- What would it take to turn this desire into a reality in my life?
- Am I willing to do what it takes to make this happen?

Sometimes, our desires can feel tucked deep inside, too far away to ever materialise. Beginning the process of manifesting these desires in your life, though, can be as simple as just acknowledging them.

You might barely scratch the surface to begin with, but the more you enquire, the more will come forward. If you're greeted with a blank, then that's a clue showing you there's deep work to do to get in touch with your desirous self. Manifesturbation™ (see pages 270–1) is a great practice for this, which you can explore by visiting us at laceyandflynn.com.

Many a person feels desire-less or as if their desires aren't even their own. When we're lacking in desire, it's not because we're inherently frigid or broken. What's probably happening is something far more profound than a label we might place on ourselves to judge or belittle what we might experience as our own inadequacies.

Whether as the result of trauma or of living a life that's completely out of alignment with what you truly value, desires can go underground and be challenging to tap into. Know you're not alone. It's not uncommon for us to work with people who say the words: 'I don't know what I want.'

For women, this is often the result of feeling like their wants, especially in the bedroom, don't matter. This then fans out into the rest of their lives, leaving them feeling confused about what they truly desire from this existence.

For men, there's often the primal want and the desire for satisfaction, but beyond scratching the itch, there can be uncertainty around a deeper level and layer of desire. In addition, male desire has been heavily shaped by pornography (see pages 232–8), so many men *think* they know what they want as a result of having seen it performed on screen. More often than not, though, their true desires are different from those depicted in pop culture, and they might feel conflicted, thinking they're 'wrong' for wanting what they want.

A woman might shave her pubic hair because she's been taught that bald is best and the mode preferred by most men. Meanwhile, her partner might actually prefer a huge muff, but since he's been shaped by porn, he doesn't want to admit it. The woman doesn't know what she actually likes best, because they both feel shameful – baldness feels juvenile, while hair seems dirty and untidy. The man's been taught that bald is best, but he has this urge – that feels shameful – to see a huge, hairy minge. What the hell are either of them to do with all this conflicting and destructive messaging?

It's quite a process to tease out one's own self from the web of the fabricated self.

We do so much in life because we think that's what we're meant to be doing. From the education we opt into, the careers we follow and the relationships we pursue, to the cars and homes we want – it's hard to discern what is our own personal desire and what is the path of what we think we're supposed to want.

Ask yourself, in the bedroom:

- What am I doing that's actually parroting the norm?
- Is it what I really want?
- When it comes to sex, am I bringing forward my desires or going along with the status quo?
- If I did what I truly wanted in the bedroom, how would my life be different?

The journey to elevated sex involves tough questions like these. Sure, you can stay where you're at, having whatever sex is already unfolding in your life (and if you're not having sex, you can stay that way, too). Ultimately, the choice is yours. And who's to say we even know what's best for you? Only you know that, and we'd be remiss if we positioned ourselves as another input in your life, urging you to go this way or that. But if you're reading this and it resonates, then you are probably ready for change.

Only you know. And to hear the voice that knows beyond doubt, beyond construct, beyond fear, you have to choose to listen within and to trust what it is you hear inside, instead of what you've been hearing your whole life from the outside world.

When you do this, you stand a chance of living the highest expression of life, which, if you're anything like us, is the reason you get up every single day: to be your whole self, to be free and to unapologetically claim your deepest desires.

From rumpy-pumpy to connected fucking

One of the best wins of this work is beginning to have deep, meaningful, elevated sex. From soul-less to soul-full sex sessions, this path will take you into realms of ecstasy and healing that you never thought possible.

Let's take a look at the mechanics, shall we?

In standard sex, the energy is focused in the pelvis. For most people, their focal point is between their legs, and on the movement of making that pussy or cock (or cock and cock, or pussy and pussy, or butt and whatever) come together and then thrust back and forth until eruption.

In elevated sex, though, the focus is on the whole being. You fuck from your heart, your pelvis, your entire body. You're no longer simply drilling your genitals together, but are moving like sexy serpents, ebbing and flowing with the totality of your bodacious bodies.

To really drive this point home (with our whole beings, and not just our willies and fannies), we want you to imagine a heat map. When you're fucking in the style of rumpy-pumpy – which is normie, basic sex that's all about the pelvis – all the heat and colour is isolated in the genitals, groin and hips. When you bring your whole body into it, the colour moves throughout the entire person. Sure, there's still epic sensation in the sexual centre, but now, there's also a connection to breath, heart, eyes and the energy that encompasses the whole being.

It's not as wanky as it sounds (or maybe it is). But the proof is in the orgasmic pudding. When the whole body is brought into the equation, the potential for pleasure increases, the sex session can often last longer, and other parts of the feeling journey are activated.

We have one technique that we call 'fucking from the heart'. We actually learned this in Flynn's parents' beach-side holiday house in Western Australia, when a friend of a friend came to give us chiropractic sessions. Little did we know that by the end of it, we'd be talking soulful sex, how to penetrate with the heart, complete with a fully clothed demo on the chiro table, with Flynn riding on the lap of the male practitioner.

Think of it this way. In standard sex, your pelvis is thrusting –
jackhammer-style – and the whole focus is on this aspect of
the body. When you fuck from your heart, you also thrust with
your chest, and arch with the full length of your spine, bringing a serpent-like action into the whole body. More body
contact is initiated, more of you is activated, and therefore
more pleasure and connection is created with your partner.

In our experience, a woman's pussy and connection to her
sexual self is opened via her heart-space. When she feels love
and connection to her partner's heart, she feels safe to open
up. Lacey has experienced this profoundly, moving from tight
and painful penetration when she's felt unseen – both by
herself and Flynn – to fully open and enjoyable deep-pussy
thrusting, when she has felt loved, safe and cherished.

The opposite seems to be true for a man. When Flynn's
sexual needs are met, when he feels satisfied and loved on
the corporeal, cock realm, his heart opens. It's like his dick is
the gateway to all the love in his body. When he feels seen
in his sexual expression, and when this is met and supported,
his heart blows wide open, radiating love on to Lacey, his
family and the world.

When a woman's heart is tended to, when she feels loved,
cared for and seen (by herself and by her partner), it's often
easier for her to open up, feel trusting and have epic sex.

When a man's cock is tended to, when he feels acknowl-
edged in his desire and satisfied physically and sexually, his
heart opens and his capacity for love emerges and expands.

It's all really rather beautiful and poetic.

Imagine this ...

A man is on the brink of orgasm and needs some help backing off (aka not blowing his load). Instead of penetrating from his cock, he starts to penetrate with his heart. Sure, his cock is still penetrating, but now he draws his energy and his focus upwards through breathing and circulates it away from the penis. The inclination towards imminent orgasm dissipates, creating room for more play and exploration.

In this fucking from the heart technique (and way of life, really), we weave together the physical with the soulful and take sex into new realms. From this space, sex becomes about so much more than an orgasm or a process to reach a destination – although there's no shame in that: a quickie for a cum still has its place in elevated sex. It's all about harmony and expressing the different energies instead of residing in one place.

Sex can be soulful, raunchy, cathartic, healing, emotional, frustrating, enlivening and every other experience possible. No longer are we interested in only showing up and doing it because we're 'in the mood' or we want the other person to turn us on. We come together from a place of self-responsibility, owning our own journeys, lit up from within and ready for a new depth of connection, where ecstasy and personal evolution are inevitable.

Your new sex, distilled

- Being your own greatest turn-on, the one to light your own fire, is paramount on your journey towards elevated sex.
- Claiming your desire will set you free from shame and help you move away from status-quo sex that isn't truly about you and what you want.
- Moving from rumpy-pumpy to connected fucking involves going into the heart, the soul, and deciding to take sex from the physical to the cosmic.
- Your emotions are welcome in the bedroom – and are, in fact, integral to feeling more pleasure and connecting more deeply, with yourself and your lover.

4

Your sexual storyline

We humans understand the world by drawing parallels and linking objects and situations to circumstances and memories. Stories and memory inform much of how we live and feel now, even if we don't realise it or consciously choose these connections. For example, a potato becomes a food of nostalgia, linking us in memory to our grandmother who harvested them by hand at the closing of summer. Beyond this conscious remembering, we also have the cellular memory from our ancestors, a deep echo in our bones and psyche taking us back to a time we can't remember but that did happen, maybe when potatoes were the only thing in the pantry during a particularly hard season when our great-great-uncle died.

No, this chapter isn't about potatoes or a weird potato fetish. This is about how your relationship to sex and intimacy is often crafted – not entirely, but substantially – by those who have come before you. We might like to believe we arrive in this world unencumbered, free of stories, perspectives and constructs, but that's not the case. Each of us comes from other humans. We're created by people who have their own histories, backgrounds, ideologies and viewpoints. In the same way, we're prone to inheriting certain physical traits from those who come before; we're also prone to inheriting ways of being in this world, and the lenses through which we see it.

Your sexual storyline is one of the most important things to unpack on your journey to elevated sex. How you arrive to sex, who you are, and what ideas, notions and experiences you carry, shape not only your relationship to sex but, ultimately, how your sexual experiences will inevitably unfold.

It's not something most of us have done – exploring the internal framework we embody and uphold when it comes to sex, intimacy, our bodies and relationships – but understanding this perhaps mysterious and slightly uncomfortable facet of yourself will be a pivotal piece in the process of you having deep, meaningful, elevated sex.

You see, you don't just arrive to sex with your own views. In fact, the views you have are probably not your own at all. We suggest it's high time you question everything.

Your relationship to sex is actually a mélange of the views and experiences of your parents, grandparents and siblings; the culture and society around you; your friends and peers; and popular culture and religion – along with a dash of your own personal experiences and those of the lovers, partners and mates you've interacted with along the way.

Whether these elements are things that have been passed down didactically, notions you picked up listening to others speak, or energies you took on – feeling them in your body as the result of someone else's unspoken embodied experience – your sexual storyline has probably been written without you as the author, and it's time to fully unpack that so you can move forward from a sexually awakened place, understanding what's shaped you and what to do about it.

Back to your start

When you were a little person, navigating your body, your desires and ultimately your sexuality for the first time, many things happened that shaped you. You might not realise these things happened, or that circumstances outside of your control created who you are now, but they did.

Throughout your life, you were shaped by the people who raised you and the people with whom you spent time. You were influenced by their views, and many of the views you hold dearly now are a direct result of the people who nurtured you (or didn't) along your path.

Now you stand here, an autonomous adult living your own life, expressing your own desires and sexuality, but how much of it is actually yours? And what experiences shaped you, for better or worse?

As parents, we're always exploring our relationships to ourselves and how these relationships are the ultimate influence on our children. What we say matters, but who we are and how we act and embody this matters even more. You can say to a child, 'Love your body,' but then if they see you admonishing your own in the mirror daily, they'll find it hard to follow your words over your actions.

The same goes for our reactions.

When we're not versed in sexual expressiveness and find our bodies shameful, or find self-touch shameful, or don't know how to navigate our own desires, we pass this on to our kids. When they touch themselves, it's easier to say what our parents said to us and recreate the cycle, than it is to pause, understand our own stories and views, and then choose differently.

How you feel about sex will impact your children (if you have them), your partner, your friends and, on an energetic level, all those you encounter.

Think back to your own parents. What was their relationship to sex like? What did they say (or not say), and how did the energy around this feel for you? It might sound simple, but this small enquiry will probably give you a lot to explore. Our parents, these beings who gave us life, also gave us their views, and this is especially true around sex.

One of the first things you can enquire into, then, is what you can remember about your parents and sex when you were a kid. Both of us have strong memories around this – our students do as well, and we bet you do, too. This is a great starting point, as these early memories put you on a course in your own life that shaped you and brought you to this moment. Whether it was something positive, negative or somewhere in the middle, there's probably some nugget in there that now informs your own relationship to sex.

Energetic inheritance

Let's get weird and go way back to a time before you existed in the shape you do now. Even if this is a far stretch for you, try to keep an open mind.

Did you know that your grandmother carried you inside her womb when she carried your mother? When your mother was developing as a foetus in utero, by about twenty weeks into the pregnancy, she would have had a fully developed reproductive system, and all the eggs in her tiny ovaries that she would ever have. Isn't that extraordinary?

Your grandmother actually carried *you* in her body – and we believe the mother cannot have an experience or feeling without the baby in her womb also having said experience.

Sceptics or those not accustomed to believing in more than the material might say there's no impact to an unborn baby, and that emotions or experiences couldn't possibly be passed down and result in a predisposition: *How could an egg, which is what you started as, experience any feelings on an embodied level?* The pregnant woman may experience a feeling, such as rejection, and share this via a chemical reaction that moves throughout her body – including the unborn child and all the potential children now existing as eggs inside that unborn child.

Inheritance runs deeper than the skin.

There's science on this, too, if you're interested in that sort of thing. You can check out epigenetics, which is the exploration of how your environment can cause changes in the functioning of your genes. Epigenetic changes begin before you're even born. Unlike genetic changes, though, epigenetic changes don't change your DNA sequence. They can be reversed, which means rewriting your storyline, for example, is possible.

In this line of enquiry and belief, who you are – or, rather, your psyche, in terms of your human mind, soul and spirit – is comprised of the experiences and feelings your ancestors and parents had. And while you're not bound to them entirely, you are predisposed towards them, and are probably more prone to experiencing and expressing certain feelings because of the historical association.

With that, it's time to question what belongs solely to you. What is your legacy or inheritance? Who are you without the experiences and lives of your ancestors?

These are monumental questions that might best be solved with psilocybin tea on a warm, dewy summer evening under a blanket of stars. We'll make an effort here, though.

There's a certain amount of relief that comes when we understand it's not all entirely up to us. How we feel, react and view the world can't be summed up by our singular experience. We are the sum of lifetimes before: our own, yes; perhaps others, if you fancy the possibility of reincarnation. But also, at the very least, the experiences of our ancestors are the blood and bones that created the fleshy forms we inhabit today.

So, if you can feel iffy about sexual advances because of your grandmother's experience while you were in utero, how might your entire sexual understanding and belief structure be impacted by this – or something that happened lifetimes before? And can anything be done to heal the past and step into a present and future that's deeply your own?

6

LACEY

I remember doing handstands in the hallway when my father left. I heard stories afterwards that his relationship with my mother ended because of a lack of sex and intimacy. I vowed somewhere within me to never be with anyone who cared so much about sex that they'd leave me because of it. I never talked to any of my grandparents about their sex lives, but I have wondered about the trajectory of sexual challenges in my family, and whether I belong to a long line of women who felt disempowered in the bedroom, like it wasn't really about them. I believe there's more to it than me. This makes it both a relief that I'm not alone in this, and also exciting, because in doing this work, I heal backwards and forwards, liberating my ancestors and creating a new path for my children and future generations.

FLYNN

I have spoken openly around the topic of sex with my parents and I feel that my story is quite clear in this area. While they would not consider themselves practitioners in the space of elevated sex, they have maintained their daily intimacy connection and a strong sexual bond that is still alive and well. I came from them – their love, their passion and their energy – and this established a strong foundation in my own sex and love life.

_____ **,** _____

Unpacking your sexual storyline

What did your parents say about sex when you were a little kid? When you 'got caught' touching yourself, what was said to you, and what feeling did it leave in your body?

Going back further, what happened with your ancestors when it came to sex? Were they religious, disembodied and prudish, or were they wild, free, totally embodied and living their best sexual lives?

We've witnessed couples of over a decade wake up to their current reality by digging into the past. Many people take a lot of responsibility for the way they are. And sure, this is important – we ought to take responsibility for ourselves and feel a certain level of empowerment when it comes to how we show up in the world.

At the same time, there's a great alleviation of responsibility, or at least a tempering, when we recognise that there are certain facets of ourselves that just aren't entirely up to us. You might take umbrage with your relentless sexual shame, flogging yourself for being so uptight and distressed when it comes to sex, but really, is this your doing? Did you choose this experience, or did it happen at some point in your life – before, during or after birth – without you having much say in the equation?

Now, let's dig into choice and what this means. We'll take another esoteric step, and hope we don't fall off the cosmic cliff, never to return to the land of the rational and linear.

In the realm of manifestation (the belief that you are, in fact, an authority with substantial say in the unfolding of your reality), we believe that your soul aligns to certain experiences. It's not that you willingly call in horrible things, or that if something bad happens to you, you asked for it. Instead, it's that you are on a path of awakening, and in order to do so, you align to experiences that facilitate growth and expansion.

Often, this element of 'bad things happening' is misunderstood when it comes to manifestation. If you can intentionally make things happen that you desire, doesn't that mean you're also making things happen that you *don't* desire?

To alleviate self-blame, we choose a different vantage point for understanding the manifestation of challenges or trauma. We choose to explore *why* the soul aligned to the experience. The idea is not that the soul called it in, but that some part of your being aligned to the experience, so something karmically was destined to come from it. As the cliché goes, *everything happens for a reason*.

We know, this is all getting a bit out there. We won't go into it any further, because this isn't a book about the subtleties of manifestation (although we are going to teach you one of our signature dishes – Manifesturbation™ – in chapter nine). But what we hope to leave you pondering right now is how you can take responsibility for your story without overly personalising it, because it wasn't entirely down to you or the choices you've made. Simultaneously, we want you to feel empowered and take responsibility from the position that this is your life: your soul aligned to this journey for some reason, and now is the moment to unpack it all and learn from it so you can grow in the direction that feels most expansive for you right now.

So, in terms of your sexual storyline, think about this: how can you own your story, not let it get heavy, then unpack, heal and release the parts that aren't serving you?

Applying ancestral, personal and cultural storylines to your sexual storyline

The layers to this are extraordinary. The palimpsest of narratives that stack and weave in order to create the sum total of who we are (or believe we are), and how we concomitantly show up in the world, is magnificent.

Imagine a figure of eight or infinity symbol. On one side are your ancestors – people you have never known but whose lives and stories are animated through you even now, perhaps without you realising it. On that same side is the rest of your family, too – your grandparents, parents, aunts, uncles and siblings. Then, on the other side, you have people like teachers, friends, past lovers. You also have culture and the world you inhabit. And at the junction in the middle, weaving it all together, you have yourself, and the events that have unfolded on a personal level to create the story of your life.

Now that you have a finer view and background, imagine this weaving together to create something that no longer has a linear presence across time and space, and instead exists all at the same time – now – in you and through you.

In unpacking your sexual storyline, you not only disentangle your relationship to pleasure and procreation, but also to the energy that created you and the energy that will create future generations. It's a healing and awakening to oneness at its core, far more powerful and all-encompassing than a simple bang in a pub loo on a Friday night (although this might also be a cosmic, timeless experience that connects you into divinity and oneness).

As you begin navigating your own relationship to sex, you can start asking yourself which beliefs are your own, and which came with you or were impressed upon you after entering this world.

You might like to write it all down and ask yourself these four questions to start. (We deal with this at length in our signature programme Sex Elevated, so if you want to go deeper, join us at laceyandflynn.com.)

• How do I feel when I think about sex?
• What do I believe to be true about sex?
• Where did these feelings and beliefs stem from?
• What would I like to believe about sex?

If you simply think about it, you'll get some benefit. But if you actually take the time to sit with it, write it all down and explore it on a deeper level, you'll receive far greater benefits, and the transformations will have more depth and longevity. The choice is yours.

You may find that you have an inkling of a memory or a feeling, and have no idea where it came from. This might seem totally far out – and if so, we get it. In today's world, we have become accustomed to only prizing rational ideas, and anything in the spiritual or energetic fields gets dubbed lesser-than or ridiculous. If you're up for challenging yourself and these notions, do it. Get weird. Go far out. Explore other realms of possibility.

Maybe your great-great-great-grandmother, who you never met, was the birthing point of a sexual storyline that cascaded through the family's narrative. Maybe you felt something inside your parents' dynamic while in utero that shaped you and the way you show up sexually. Or maybe something happened when you were a kid – something was said, hinted at or observed – that then influenced all your thoughts and feelings around sex and sexuality.

You might remember without remembering. You might know something without proof. And this isn't about drudging up the past or looking for excuses or reasons. Instead, it's about opening yourself up to the interconnectedness of it all, and the possibility that you are more than you, and there are so many cool angles from which to view yourself and understand yourself.

When diving into this subject, it can also be very healing to have some conversations with your parents or relatives to try and piece together some of this story. Start softly and ask broad questions, and go step by step. If things are going well, you can ask more pointed questions? Be the sex detective in this moment, because the more you can piece together your family's story, the more you can understand your own.

If there's stuff that you can't quite put your finger on that irks or haunts you, you may need the support of a professional to help you clear historical patterns or unpack this further in a safe space. This work – here in the book, with us in a programme or coaching container, or with another professional – can pay huge dividends, not only by clearing remnants of stuck energy, but also by offering you a feeling of liberation at having finally shifted these storylines, putting you more in control of your life, and ensuring you are not perpetuating this stuck energy for those that come after you.

Your sexual storyline, distilled

- Your ancestors, your family, this culture and your own experiences influence your unique life.
- Everything in life has memories and stories attached to it, even sex. Understanding your sexual storyline will help set your sex free.
- It's likely your family and ancestral storylines are impacting how you fuck now. It's time to dig into this so that you understand yourself better.

- Reviewing your personal experiences with sex throughout your life will help you come to terms with any current issues and challenges you're facing in the bedroom.
- For better or worse, we're not in this alone. Looking back can be key to healing deeply and ultimately creating an elevated sex life going forward.

5

How to talk about sex

Communication is king and queen when it comes to the bedroom. But this isn't just about the words you speak, although they are paramount. This is about communicative attunement, understanding your body and your partner's body, paying attention to the tone of your voice and knowing how to read energy – ultimately, becoming an expert on all facets of connecting.

Because let's face it: sex is communication.

It's verbal and non-verbal, it's emotional and energetic – in its entirety, it's about expressing needs, wants and desires. So it goes without saying that becoming an expert communicator leads the way to becoming an expert lover. And if you're rocking it at both sex and communication, and all the ways in which these two expressions weave together, you're going to have a pretty epic life, ripe with rich connection, pleasure and an overflowing of abundance.

But let's be fully honest and transparent here from the get-go: most people are absolutely shit communicators.

Maybe you're one of them yourself; if so, we're not mad at you. We get it. We've been there, too. Flynn used to get so irked at having to say a word – a single word – during sex in order to navigate what was happening, and Lacey used to find it nearly impossible to identify what she was feeling, let alone express it, when it came to all the challenges that were arising in our sex life. In addition, Flynn used to tout himself as a horrible communicator when it came to the spoken and written word – and now, here he is, working as a coach, writing a book and sharing his ideas with the world. We can all change, not only in action, but in our views of ourselves, which is half the journey to actually embodying and activating change.

So, if communication is more than just hearing someone say something and then saying something back, what exactly *is* communication? And, more to the point, what is *elevated* communication?

Glad you asked.

Elevated communication is an embodied experience meaning that all faculties of the body are online and activated. It's not just ears and mouth, although your ears and mouth are great assets. It's an expression of your whole sensory body. Elevated communication is about attuning, observing, feeling, embodying, thinking and expressing from a place of groundedness in yourself and connection to the other.

So much of the communication you're part of now is probably reaction-based, meaning that you hear or witness, then react. It's not necessarily born of presence, or a connection to yourself or the other. It's more a ping-pong match of ideas and experiences, rallied back and forth.

We all grow up spending our lives never truly listening, centring ourselves in every conversation, wanting to be right, all while usually missing the deepest point of communication: to connect, to witness and be seen, and to have something new be born of any given exchange.

Half the time, we're so in our own heads when we're communicating – trying to figure out how the conversation relates to us, having a memory triggered and wanting to share it, or worrying about our place in the conversation – that we're not truly present or tuned in to the intricacies and subtitles of the exchange. From the white noise of superficial chitchat, to people who talk without listening (and people who listen without talking), we've got some problems with communication.

It's no secret that the two of us have some pretty strong views on the state of affairs when it comes to humans relating with one another. And of course, it's not all dire. There are extraordinary connections happening every moment of every day. What we want to ensure, though, is that more conscious connections start happening, both in and out of the bedroom, helping people feel more deeply heard, understood and, ultimately, connected – to themselves and to one another.

The basics of elevated communication, in and out of the bedroom

Communication is defined as exchanging information – and at its most basic, yes, that's what it's about. It's about sharing yourself and your truth with someone else. But the ways in which you do that successfully are open to exploration.

What most people don't know is that masculine and feminine communication styles differ dramatically. Men who identify with the masculine usually communicate to solve problems. It's less about exploration and more about finding a solution. Meanwhile, women who identify with the feminine tend to meander with communication, discovering themselves through the process of sharing. Those with a feminine essence communicate to express while those with a masculine essence communicate to resolve. One is based on the journey, while the other is based on a destination.

Remember, we all embody both energies, so of course women can be clear-cut and men can explore. On the whole, though, the core of masculine and feminine communication styles connect to the individual essence of the person, and the essence defines how that person is most likely to show up in dialogue and verbal communication.

Knowing this, you can begin to see the implications of two people with very different styles of communication trying to find common ground and mutual understanding. This is where understanding the motive behind dialogue is imperative. If you want to chat to find a solution, then stating that is helpful. Similarly, if you want to connect in order to share, express and explore without the need for a tidy end result, stating that from the outset can be quite helpful too.

Bringing your body online

Epic communication requires knowing yourself. It's not about a preservation of your smaller self, but a tuning in to your highest self so that you can really be available to the full experience of any given exchange.

Think about how exciting communication truly is (and please, allow us to be total nerds about this). During a communicative event, you're having an exchange with another autonomous being on planet Earth. The fact that both of you are here together, in this moment, is nothing short of miraculous; depending on your belief system or spiritual inclination, it's the result of some pretty fantastic synchronistic happenstances. So, just as a starting point, the sheer epicness of getting the chance to relate to and with another being in this way is phenomenal.

You might need to take off your jaded shades if this feels far-fetched for you, because restoring your *joie de vivre* is something we're interested in doing through the *Come Together* process. We want you to come together with your delight, your possibility mindset and your truest turned-on nature, lit up by the magic of the mundane happening all around you, to you and for you.

If you let yourself be lit up by the normal nature of this extraordinary existence, you'll become a happier human, a more alive lover and an all-around elevated person. It's win-win.

And listen, we know you thought this was all about sex. Let us remind you: it is. Because, as you'll remember, sex is everything. It's the foundation of your life and it's the expression of your truest creative energy. It's *everything*. So to bring yourself into your fullest capacity for sexual expression, you're going to have to become the fullest version of yourself in the process – and this version has all the time in the world for expanding into the possibilities, the delight and the potential for happiness and feeling in this life.

So, back to that deeply grounded and simultaneously cosmic experience that is having the opportunity to communicate with another being ...

How can you show up in full respect and reverence for both yourself and the other in this situation? How can you give this opportunity for soulful connection the presence it deserves?

Because it's far more important than sitting there, scrolling on your phone, checking out, half-listening and chiming in with minutiae that's below you. This is a moment for something profound, even if you're simply listening to how someone's day has gone. You have the opportunity to hear what they're saying, and also to hold space for what they're not saying: what they're feeling, what their body is expressing, and even what they haven't awoken to yet in themselves, but you can sense and witness because you're such a tuned-in and available human. Boom.

Co-listening and holding space

Teaching this process is a highlight of our work. It's been fundamental on our own journey, teaching us both how to be more present, tuned in and available to the truth of the moment (and also to actually hear one another, and speak openly and freely beyond superficial conversing).

This technique is all about learning to be fully there for someone, beyond your own needs in the moment, and beyond your own need to chime in, be heard or be right. It's the ultimate path of cultivating both the witness and the listener in both people. And it's also the ultimate path to learning how to truly share your inner world, without input, validation or immediate reflection from your partner.

Let's get this straight, though: this is not about bypassing yourself in favour of prioritising the other person. Elevated sex is never, ever about that, and neither is elevated, whole-heart communication. You aren't abandoning yourself or dissociating from your needs in order to give someone else what they need. Instead, you're allowing space for your needs to exist, as they always do, but you're not focusing on your needs in this moment, you're focusing on the needs of the other. If, however, the needs of the other cross a boundary for you, then this is something we'll need to address.

Remember, every part of this process is about consensually showing up in your fullest expression, as your highest self, in service to you, your vision and your desires. So, if you're engaged in this practice, for example, and the person is saying things that are aggressive, with the intention to harm, making you feel unsafe, this isn't a moment for you to prioritise the other person. However, if the person is taking radical responsibility and sharing their perspective, but their perspective happens to offend you or rub your ego the wrong way – well that's another story.

Here are two scenarios where a person wants to share their dissatisfaction around kissing. One demonstrates self-responsibility and is a great opportunity to co-listen and hold space, while the other feels aggressive and lacking self-responsibility. Note and feel the difference ...

Whole-heart communication I'm feeling awkward about the way we kiss. It feels too wet for me sometimes. I find myself withdrawing because I don't know how to deal with it. I want to be able to kiss you freely, but I get scared. I'd love to change something, but I don't know what.

Aggressive communication The way you kiss grosses me out. I really can't stand it any more. You're sloppy, the kisses are too wet and I just want to throw you off me whenever you get like that. Why can't you just be a better kisser?

Notice that the first scenario doesn't tiptoe around the issue, but conveys the message clearly, without cruelty. The first scenario offers feedback, whereas the second offers criticism. One is heart-centred, whereas the other is mean-spirited and lacks self-responsibility.

If you find yourself experiencing aggressive communication during this practice, or regularly in your relationship, this is not right. If speaking about it with your partner doesn't help, it might be time to seek outside support. If you ever feel afraid, unsafe or in danger, it's imperative you find help and appropriate support.

You need to become clear on the nuances of your experience. There needs to be space for you to not like what's being said or shared, but instead of reacting or centring your own experience, it's important to allow yourself to hold the space for the other person. It's powerful, it's new, and yes, it can be challenging. But you're up for it, because you're a devotee to the path of elevated sex, thriving relationships and being your most epic self.

This practice of co-listening and holding space is something you can bring into your dating life or relationship right away. It might feel a bit awkward or strange at first, but with practice, it might just become one of the most profound ways you express, share with and hear your partner, enabling you to understand their experiences, feelings and thoughts – on any number of facets of life, but most notably, on your sex and intimate life.

Take note: this journey is best taken outside the heat of the moment. So, if you're having a blow-up, it's not usually the best time to have a spontaneous session (although feel free to prove us wrong and give it a go). We've found, though, for both ourselves and our clients, that it's best to make this a mutually decided-upon exercise that you co-create at a pre-determined moment in time. Just as we learn how to schedule sex and intimacy on the path of elevated sex, we also learn how to do any number of practices that lead the way to a thriving relationship. And this is a cornerstone practice.

All you need is quiet space, twenty minutes and the willingness to show up fully. You'll also need a timer or clock.

How to do it

Decide first who will be the speaker and who will be the listener. We usually give an arbitrary guideline for this, so nobody needs to volunteer for either position. For example, the person with the longer hair can be the listener first, and the person with the shorter hair can be the speaker. If this is too tough to call, flip a coin. Once you've decided your roles, sit back-to-back, facing in opposite directions. This means that your bodies are connected, but you're facing away from each other.

The reason we start facing in opposite directions is that it gives each person ample space to be with themselves, while also being connected with one another. Sure, you can start off staring into one another's eyes and getting right into the centre of connection and intimacy, but the path we're suggesting here offers a gentler lead-in, especially if this is new to you. Plus, we find it's generally easier to fully share and let flow all your deepest meanderings when you're not looking right at the other person. You can move on to doing this face to face once you've done the practice a couple of times, or you can stick with this approach if it feels aligned.

Once you're in position, you're going to set the timer for seven minutes. The speaker will then hit 'go' and share for said seven minutes. You can decide on a topic to start, like the current state of your sex life or a specific challenge you're facing, and then you can let flow all your ideas and feelings for that entire seven minutes.

The listener: holding space and witnessing

During this time, the listener is simply listening. And what does that mean? It means witnessing, hearing, listening intently and holding space. Holding space means keeping the container open so the other person can explore and discover themselves. Honestly, it's an opportunity to put yourself in your partner's shoes and understand the way they feel.

This experience of co-listening and holding space is not conversation. It's not a dialogue but a practice in listening and sharing, meaning both partners have a chance to be both listener and listened-to.

As the person who holds space, you have a unique position, in that your job is to be available, without judgement, without ever acting upon your own momentary need to chime in. If you find yourself trying to fix the issue, wanting to pipe up with your thoughts, or getting irked for some reason about what you're hearing, you're going to breathe and remember that your main intention is to be there, to fully hear and bear witness to the experience of your lover.

You're not there to fix. You're there to understand.

Remember in chapter three, when we talked about depersonalising situations, not making it about you and instead allowing it to be about the other person entirely? This is another feature of that. What we want you to discover is that being a present listener is, in fact, super healing for both the listener and the listened-to. You don't have to know anything or fix the other person or give any feedback. Your only role is to be there, fully there; to witness and hold the space with love and integrity.

The speaker: radical self-responsibility vs projecting

As the speaker, your role is to fully share and let flow on the decided-upon topic. You want to avoid projecting on to the other person and instead to claim ownership over your experiences, ideas and feelings. This is when whole-heart communication comes into play, which we'll speak about more in a moment. You don't want to blame or be right, either. You want to express from your heart what it is you're feeling, how it's impacting you and the journey you're on.

Of course, the other person is a part of this, and they'll probably factor into the sharing in one way or another, but this practice is about full self-responsibility. This is how you begin to move on from some of the challenges and problems we unpacked in chapter three, and into a more elevated, mature and thriving union.

So, now that you're both clear on your roles, with the timer set, you can begin. The listener never needs to say anything or make a sound. They breathe, tune in to their ears and heart, and hold the space. The speaker lets flow everything that's inside of them from a place of self-responsibility and personal power.

If the speaker feels stumped or shy, they breathe and continue. It's fine to say the words, 'I don't know what to say.' Try to keep talking, even when you get a bit stuck. Say why you're stuck. For example, 'I'm trying to think of things to say, but I keep feeling ashamed. I can't quite say what it is . . .' and keep going.

Part of the journey for the speaker is becoming self-aware and recognising what it is they're experiencing inside that might impact their ability to speak freely. It might seem simple – and let's be honest, you'll probably even be tempted to read this and then never do it. We all love to take in information and not activate it (remember resistance?). But unless you actually initiate and embody the work through action, you will not experience the change. You will have a whole lot of theory upstairs in your noggin, and very little actual transformation and elevation in your physical life.

Always remember, sex is of the body.

You can't think your way to elevated sex. You can't read your way to an epic, thriving relationship. At some point, it all has to come online via your body. So if not now, then when? And if not you, then who? This is your life. This is your love. This is your desire, your pleasure, your healing and your thriving. Take a deep breath and give it a go. And if you're not going to do it now, put it in your calendar now and make a date with your person so you remain accountable for following through.

If there's no lover currently in your life with whom you can – or want – to do this, do it with a friend. This is an epic practice to bring your relationship closer together. If you're comfortable with the person, you can still talk about sex and intimacy and work together to unpack a shared view. It's all in the service of you and your evolution, so however you can activate the work, do it. You're worth it.

Whole-heart communication

All this talk about sex begs a deep dive into love, doesn't it? Because do elevated sex and epic intimacy even exist without love?

The short answer is no, they don't.

Even if you're not in love with the person you're screwing around with, you can remember that love is a way of being in the world, instead of just a feeling you have and direct towards a specific individual.

Many insightful spiritual teachers across the ages have taught that true love is an embodied experience that brings the individual into rapture: not necessarily a sexual, religious or even spiritual rapture, but instead a rapture of true and pure love felt in every fibre of our being.

Maybe you've heard someone say before that love is our natural state. Everything else is an illusion. Imagine if this were true. Imagine if below the anger, the hurt, the pain, the jadedness – imagine if under the surface of your uncertainty and lack of confidence, there was actually a well of overflowing love waiting to be tapped in to.

Instead of sticking with the same old that isn't actually working for most of us when it comes to feeling sustainably joyful, sexually alive and content in our lives, perhaps it's time to start thinking and feeling in fresh ways.

The truth is, we've all become accustomed to a life of grinding, devoid of ease and lightness. And when you grind something, eventually it turns into nothing. Grinding is the reduction of something, or else an oppressive experience that never seems to end (although when we get to the reclamation of language on pages 155–6, we'll talk about how saying grinding when it comes to boning is actually totally cool – but we're on a flow right now, so let's go with it). So if we're all living these grinding lives, wearing ourselves down, using too much force and excessive energy all the time, for everything, we're all going to end up tired and jaded. Maybe you can relate?

We've been at this place – individually and as a couple – countless times over the many years of our relationship. Trying to figure it out, forcing sex on to both our bodies when it wasn't aligned, doing jobs that weren't right, and just *doing*, relentlessly doing, as a way of being that felt like all there was to this life.

LACEY

Even though I was in love with Flynn, sex didn't feel like making love; it felt confusing and painful. In the early days, it was the stuff of love, yes, but still, my inner world was in conflict. There was so much in my storyline that corrupted the natural unfolding of sex that, eventually, I could scarcely have it. I wasn't adept at expressing myself when it came to this avenue of life, either, so I just shut down, got emotional and felt under threat.

FLYNN

There was a time when we didn't have the words or skill set to talk about what was happening. We also didn't have the full aware- ness that what was happening was a problem. It was a strange in-between after the honeymoon phase. Lacey was often in pain – we both knew it – but we didn't know it was a problem. It felt like a problem, because it created issues for us, but because it was also somehow normalised in society, this idea of women enjoying sex less than men, it seemed like what we were feeling was at odds with the status quo. This is a very important moment, and it's one that a lot of people find themselves in. That moment of realisation and awakening to the truth beyond the storyline. We thought it was physical and that Lacey had a 'small, shallow, not very deep' pussy. We thought, 'This is just the way it is.' But our higher selves knew better. Eventually, we'd go from having sex where Lacey's body was on eggshells, in pain and in contraction, to Lacey being totally in charge, capable of fucking from every angle. It was never her body that was 'broken'. It was the way she'd embodied – the way we'd all embodied – not tending to women's true needs and all the ways in which men and women differ in the bedroom. But without words for this, without the ability to talk and listen, identify the truth and share it, people get stuck. We were stuck in painful sex for years, but once we woke up and did the work, we came out the other side, able to fuck pain-free at full depth, from every angle.

So, what does any of this have to do with whole-heart communication?

Elevated sex isn't possible without love, and in order to surmount the disconnect that so many of us are facing – in our bodies, in our lives and, subsequently, in the bedroom – love has to be initiated and embodied as a state of being.

We have to find enough love for ourselves that we're willing to heal. We have to calibrate our actions to love so that fear, hate, self-loathing and unworthiness no longer motivate us on a conscious or subconscious level. We have to choose the path of the devoted lover, loving ourselves and showing love to those we choose to fuck.

Because you don't have to be in love to share love, and you don't need to be in love to be lovers. Love is the energy that underpins the expression of elevated sex. Sure, there's also desire, pleasure, lust, longing, the animalistic urges of the rewilded human. It's all there. But the current that connects it all must be love.

Whole-heart communication is a way of expressing yourself that flows from the heart. First, you become centred in your heart as the anchorage of your life. Your words are soaked through your heart before they're born from your mouth. You check in with your heart to make sure your actions and words are in integrity with your truth and expressed with compassion for self and other.

Let's get this straight, though: this doesn't mean you have to become some wanky poet only spouting tender nothings (although if that's you, then we don't think you're wanky – we think you're being you, and that's awesome, keep going). What we mean is that this isn't a performance. We still want you to be raunchy if you're raunchy. We want you to skank it, be hilarious, get nasty, be yourself. Let your freak flag fly. If it's you, it's in the heart, and no preconceived image of a whole-heart lover needs to usurp the truth of who you are.

Instead, this is about using your love-space, your heart, as the central axis for your communication. It's yogic science and philosophy – the heart is actually the bridge between the lower and higher realms. Below the heart, you have three centres, and above the heart, you have three more. The heart is the meeting point, merging the lower will with the higher powers of the individual. Let this move and inspire you. Let your heart be the meeting point in your body where everything comes through.

All of this sounds great in theory, but what does this actually mean in practice? How do you activate love in your life?

This is a simple practice, and one you can begin doing right now, in this moment. Before you act, when you find yourself at a crossroads, or when you are in the midst of struggle, battling internally with yourself or externally with your lover, ask yourself:

What would love do right now?

The answer might not come straight away. It might be more of a prayer to begin with – and a prayer that doesn't come with an easy answer. But as you become more attuned to your heart, the answers will become more readily available, louder and quicker to slide right into the centre of your being.

You can place your hands on your heart, drop those stressed-out shoulders, soften that tired mind that's been running endlessly trying to figure it all out, and simply ask yourself: What would love do right now?

You'll probably find that things become clear for you quite quickly – and if they don't, don't worry. Just keep opening yourself to being a channel for clear sight so that you can arrive at your own conclusions based on what's truly right for you, in the heart place, with love as your guiding force.

Here's how to put 'What would love do?' into action during sex

Say you're having sex and having a hard time connecting with yourself and your partner. You're starting to get really annoyed with yourself. Your mind is fuming; you're berating yourself for being inept at relaxing, opening up and simply enjoying sex. This is a great moment to ask yourself: 'What would love do?'.

- In this moment, how can love lead the way and encourage you to treat yourself with kindness?
- Instead of getting annoyed with yourself, how can love towards yourself soften the situation and promote healing instead of contraction?

Or say you really want to do it doggy style, and your partner instantly shuts you down. You feel hurt, so you start closing your heart. In this moment, take a breath and ask yourself, 'What would love do?'.

- Can expanding into love allow you to feel safe in yourself and not take this rejection personally?
- Does asking this question encourage you to pause the session and have a conversation that needs having?

Power language

Let's get to the fun stuff, shall we?

A client once said to Lacey, 'The way you say "pussy" is life-changing. I want to be able to do that.' What she was referring to was the energy behind the word, and what it brought forward for her.

You see, language is arguably the most powerful tool we have when it comes to communication. And this is coming from two people who prize embodiment and embodied expression above all, so it's a big claim we're making.

The thing is, that language allows us to be self-reflective, then formulate ideas and verbalise them with nuance so that others might understand our exact positioning.

Language also has the power to actually create the world. When we name something, we create it. Perhaps it already existed before the naming, but with naming – an object, an idea or an experience – it is defined. The word has a shared and mutually understood meaning, and so when we use that word, we, as a people, enter into an agreement that we are all speaking about the same thing.

With that, language becomes this extraordinary set of symbols that define and create the entire world we inhabit, all the experiences we have and how we express our innermost worlds. It goes without saying, then, that language is truly powerful. And as far as we're concerned, it's also very limited. But that's not going to stop us from giving it its credence and digging into all the ways in which language can be levelled up to support an elevated sex life and an elevated relationship.

You and your body

What words do you use to define your sexual centre? More to the point, what word do you use for your genitals? And when you say that word, how does it make you feel?

Take a moment to practise it now.

Go on, say the word out loud. If you're on the train or sitting next to your mum on the couch, you can say it in your head. But try practising it out loud later, when you're flying solo. This is the starting point for how the language you use impacts your experience of the thing you're speaking about. More on that later.

When you say the word – vagina, vulva, pussy, cunt, peach, froufrou, or penis, cock, dick, schlong, willy or johnson – how do you feel? If you had to talk about your body and refer to your genitals in front of others, would you be able to do this from an elevated place where you didn't feel shame, discomfort or awkwardness?

The reason we ask is that we find the words people use to define their genitals and the way people feel when they use said lingo is a pretty strong initial indicator of how this person actually feels about this aspect of themselves.

And why does this matter? Well, because if you can't talk about your sexual body, how are you ever going to ask for what you want, or express your needs, concerns and insights, without feeling some level of discomfort?

Elevated sex is all about healing every last vestige of shame and discomfort so that you can fully inhabit your life and feel total empowerment when it comes to all things sex and intimacy.

With that, it's time to usher in some power language for the realm between your thighs.

Power language is the term we've given to language that's been intentionally chosen to represent topics, experiences or aspects of the self. The words often go beyond surface-level description in that they harness all levels: the energetic, the physical, the emotional and the spiritual. These words, terms and turns of phrase have been dusted off from being derogatory or shameful, salvaged from having little nuance or potency, then reclaimed and spoken in a way that's charged with power and intention.

We take words that have been used to oppress, hurt or mis-represent, and we say them loud and proud from a place of empowerment and self-awareness, with just a touch of 'Fuck the system that says these words are shameful, dull or bland, or just downright wrong.'

For example, we're avid users of the words 'pussy' and 'cock'. These words are not words you often hear spoken on the playground when parents are having a chat while their toddlers go down the slide, or in therapeutic settings when someone is trying to heal their relationship to sex or intimacy.

However, in our lives, we found it imperative to disrupt and move on from the words we'd been using before we chose to live a life dedicated to elevated sex.

To be totally frank, vagina and penis weren't cutting it any more. Who wants to have their vagina caressed or penis sucked? (Added to which, 'vagina' is often totally misused, as it's actually the muscular canal leading from the vulva, or external genitals, to the cervix.)

These words – penis and vagina – had been the ones we'd been taught to say all our lives when referring to our bodies. And words like pussy and cock? Well, these were dirty terms, reserved for porn and naughty people – or else words nobody knew you said, but maybe you whispered them, with a hint of shame but a huge desire to claim them, into your partner's ear while getting down and sexy.

When we first began the dance of disentangling our sexual narratives, we decided to unpack all our associations to the words we used to define our genitals. This started with Lacey's journey.

------------- 6 -------------

LACEY

I didn't realise I felt so much shame around having a woman's body. I suppose because women grow up feeling like second-class citizens, and because our vulvas are in stark opposition to the feminine beauty standards set out for us by the world, I had a skewed view of my pussy (I'll be saying pussy from here on out, as it's the most natural and true word for me). There I was, about to give birth, calling in a profoundly independent birth experience, and I had little to no cultivated relationship with my pussy – the gateway through which my baby would leave my body and come into the world. How was I to trust this part of my body if I hadn't connected with her? How was I to come into full connection if she didn't even have a word associated with her that felt empowering? I knew I had work to do, so I started to do it.

------------- 9 -------------

In the months leading up to birth, Lacey would look at her pussy with a mirror every day. By doing this, she got to know her body in new ways (we'll tell you all about this in the next chapter). But for now, in reference to the point at hand, she realised that without a word to define her sexual centre, she couldn't speak about her body in a way that felt activated, alive and powerful.

She started playing with different words.

LACEY

At first, 'pussy' felt too sexual and a bit pornographic. Also, it was often used as a term to offend when trying to take someone down a peg and insult their strength or masculinity. At first, I was whispering the word, but after some practice I could say it just as easily as I'd say words like 'pasta' or 'sweatshirt'. It rolled right off my tongue, and women said it felt different to the way they've heard it said before. It made them bristle, sure, because it was charged and had negative connotations, but it also made them feel curious and excited, drawing something out of them that they too wanted to cultivate and harness.

By claiming this word, I took back the power of my sexual centre. I no longer felt shame, awkwardness or fear around my vulva; I felt enlivened. I had a pussy! And she wasn't simply anatomical. She was energetic and spiritual – an all-out multi-dimensional facet of my being. She became the proudest part of my body. The part I wanted to heal, love and connect with the most. And partly because of this choice to claim a word, I had an epic birth and began the phenomenal journey of healing my relationship to sex and our sex life as a couple.

Claiming a power word for your genitals

In order to speak freely about your body, you'll need to claim a word that feels empowering for you. Sure, you might love 'vagina' or 'penis', and if so, then that's cool. You do you. But if you say either of these words and feel uneasy, or there's some power missing, then it's time to do the work to heal this barrier to naming your bits.

You've already explored saying it out loud; the next step is to understand, on a deeper level, the associated thoughts. For example, you might realise you hate saying 'vagina' because whenever it was said in your family, it was to tell you not to touch it. Or maybe when it comes to the word 'penis', you can remember someone in your life saying it from a position of disease and shame, which was then passed on to you.

You'll remember we went in deep around your sexual storyline in chapter four. This is an extension of that work, but now we're doing it on a micro level, around language. This might seem tedious, doing all this 'work', but remember what's at stake: an elevated sex life, gorgeously fulfilling intimacy and pleasure beyond your wildest dreams. Pretty good reason to show up for yourself, hey?

Try answering these questions to see what comes to mind:

- What's the word you typically use to define your genitals?
- What associations do you have with this word?
- What words make you bristle?
- What words make you want to explore more?
- What word do you want to try using from here on out?

Sure, when you need to talk about your genitals in an environment that's not conducive to power language (you know, like when you're getting a check-up), you don't have to be like, 'Hey doc, can you look at my schlong? There's a bit of a bump on there that I'm not sure about.' Although, hey – if you say it in integrity, it might blow the doctor's mind.

Generational healing

There are times when using easily understood language is the discerning thing to do. With that in mind, we'll tell you how we've taught our kids about language, so you can see the path to generational healing.

When we were first navigating all this, we wanted to make sure we both protected and elevated our children in the process. It might feel empowering for a young child to say 'pussy', but out in the world at large, this could pose problems with other people who haven't done this level of work, have negative connotations around certain words, or else are prone to sexualising children. You have to be empowered and healed to get it. If you're not, then you just project your shit on to others. That's not what kids need, ever.

We decided to use the words 'vulva' and 'penis' in our family, and to use all the correct anatomical terms. We also chose to imbue the language with love, care and honesty. Our children are both capable of comfortably speaking about and referring to their bodies, because we've set the tone for a shame-free, open space where their bodies are natural, perfect and desiring of care and attention.

‘

FLYNN

Our daughter hears Lacey say 'pussy' in her work, and we've explained to her why she does this. She seems satisfied with our answers, and often smiles when she hears it used, but she doesn't usually use it herself. If she ever chose to use it, then we'd have a conversation around this to keep her safe and empowered, free from shame and also free from the projections and misunderstanding of others. Our son isn't quite old enough for this yet, but in time we'll do the same with him. At the time of writing, he's two and a half years old. He can comfortably talk about his penis and is already on the path, at this young age, to living a life where his sexual centre is normalised and integrated into his full relationship with his body and self.

’

Freeing the voice – sexual and vocal expression

Our final exploration on the journey to elevated communication is about your voice and how you use it, how it resonates, and your experience of your voice as it leaves your body and is received into the world.

Your voice – the actual feeling of it and sound of it – is an important part of this journey. When you can fully express yourself in the bedroom, you can bet your bottom dollar you'll be able to more freely express yourself at work, with your family and with every other person with whom you interact.

Speaking up during sex can be very challenging. What we have to heal and overcome in order to express our needs, desires, thoughts and feelings in this space is immense.

Our first deep dive, then, is going to be exploring the performative tendencies we all have when it comes to expressing our sexual pleasure.

Performance, authentic expression and holding back

Men tend to go into a pared-back or else monotonous space when it comes to expressing their sexual pleasure through sound. There's nothing wrong with a deep, manly grunt, but when it doesn't have any variance, it's good to explore why.

Men have typically been taught to hold back from being overly expressive. Their emotions are on lockdown, their ability to freely communicate is inhibited and their range of expressiveness during sex and pleasure is stunted. But men have a huge capacity for sexual expression that needs to be tapped in to.

Typical masculine sex sounds

We once worked with a male client inside a premium coaching container where we both coached him together. We explored what it was that held him back from fully inhabiting and expressing his sexual pleasure range.

What he discovered, through both talk and embodiment work, was that he hadn't experienced a representation of masculine pleasure that was authentic, powerful and in integrity. Up until his time working with us, he'd been reliant on porn as stimulation for his self-pleasure sessions. In the bulk of the porn he'd been watching, men were often commanding, not very expressive in their pleasure, and not always in integrity with how they were showing up and participating in the sexual dynamic.

Through coaching, he came to the conclusion that he viewed sexual expressiveness and pleasure sounds as belonging to the realm of women and the feminine. It just felt too feminine to be expressive in this way, and that was not aligned with how he viewed himself as a man.

We began to unpack this through guided journeys. He was encouraged to touch his own body, without porn, and explore the sounds that might want to be released. What he discovered, besides the epic pleasure and orgasmic release possible when not engaged with pornographic visual stimulation (see chapter six for more on self-sex), was his own powerful, masculine voice.

He'd been struggling with what masculinity meant, having been raised in a family culture where this energy felt oppressive and dangerous due to his father's erratic temper. He didn't want to perpetuate that, so he stayed on the softer side, inhabiting neither his masculine nor feminine sides fully. What he found through vocal expressiveness and self-touch was that he could truly embody his own brand of masculinity, and be super powerful and sexually charged, without feeling like this was putting him into the realm of the feminine or the aggressive masculine.

It can be a bit challenging to understand the whole discussion around feminine and masculine energies. These topics have been made rather taboo, or else are considered old-fashioned, with public discourse not wanting to pigeonhole people based on their genders or sex. We tapped into this briefly in chapter one, and we'll get into it again in chapters seven and eight. What we want to address now, though, is that when we say 'masculine' and 'feminine', we're not talking about some contract that says, 'Wear this, act like that and show up in this particular way in your life in order to play the role of your gender defined by your sex.' No, we're talking about something far more powerful, old (not old-fashioned, but ancient) and helpful. In this instance, with our client, he identifies with masculinity – with being a man, a provider, a leader. These are all inherent qualities of the masculine. But because these qualities have been used with poor intentions for many, many years, men don't know how to be men in a way that feels powerful without being dominating or oppressive.

He realised this was all tied to the way he showed up vocally in sex. His identity was actually drawn into the mix when it came to showing up and making pleasure sounds.

- Is making noise only for the feminine?
- Do men make noises other than grunts?
- As a man, what noises are my natural noises?

With this level of questioning, and never having done the work to unpack it, understand it and ultimately bring the enquiry online via the body, it was no wonder he was lost (alongside the majority of men we work with and talk to about the subject).

It was epic to witness him come into his masculine power. The sounds he learned to express by being true to himself, and the way he began to move and hold his body, were inspiring. He went from being not sure of who he was as a man, to being an embodied, sexually lit-up man who felt aligned with himself and his needs. He became his best self: an elevated man, having elevated sex and showing up in the world as he never had before. This lead him to take up new hobbies and travel internationally on trips he'd been dreaming of. He even got a woman pregnant who'd had fertility issues her whole life (but that's another story).

Flynn's voice story

When Flynn began unpacking his relationship to his voice, he realised he'd spent his whole life believing he had an unpleasant voice, one that nobody wanted to hear. He'd developed a deep voice early on in his adolescence, and as a result, he'd always felt like an outcast, someone who was targeted by teachers in school because of the tenor of his voice.

He realised through his elevated sex work that this had impacted his ability to be expressive in the bedroom. He held his voice back and didn't even know what his true pleasure sounds – beyond the standard grunt or mini-moan – actually felt like or sounded like. There was a filter there that needed to be explored.

In sex, he actually found it difficult to make noise. Even when he actively chose to, or was encouraged by Lacey, it was like there was a divide between what he was experiencing and the sound that might accompany this experience.

FLYNN

This is something that first came up on an early episode of our podcast, *Lacey & Flynn Have Sex*. Honestly, it's still something I'm unpacking, as it has been a storyline I've been running with for my whole adult and teen life. My connection to my voice, how to create and identify my authentic sound, how I'm breathing while using my voice, singing, holding back on certain sounds – it's all work that I am now focused on. I know in this space there are breakthroughs and lessons for me that will affect the rest of my life.

Typical feminine sex sounds

Women tend to have a very different problem. They're expected to be vocal and to demonstrate their pleasure at every turn. If they're not making sounds, then there's something wrong. Their pleasure sounds are meant to signal their satisfaction, putting their (usually) male counterparts at ease.

This level of pressure has often meant performing their pleasure sounds. In addition, visual representations in porn and the media perpetuate this by showcasing women making high-pitched sounds throughout every part of the sexual journey.

The truth is, though, that most women have never come into contact with their authentic voices, in the bedroom or otherwise. They not only feel disconnected from showing up and saying what they want with clarity and conviction, they articulate their pleasure from a place of pastiche, mimicking what they've seen done without even realising that it's not a true expression.

Let's get clear: this isn't blame or judgement. Sometimes we mistake a strong stance as a judgement. This isn't that. Instead, it's a unequivocal understanding of the challenges many women face.

In a rage-release workshop Lacey conducted inside a group coaching programme exclusively for women, students were guided on a journey to release anger and rage in their bodies. Part of the process was connecting to guttural screams and roars. The feedback was unanimous: the majority of the women had never made sounds like that. Some hadn't even been that loud or that vocal since childhood, some five decades prior.

Feminine performance tells us to stay high-pitched and pleasing. But true feminine pleasure? It can be guttural and growly, with grunts and moans aplenty. There's no blueprint. And if there was, this would be another opportunity for creating performative sexual expression based on an external representation instead of something truly embodied, connected and authentic.

In a nutshell, the only way into your authentic expression is to do it yourself.

You can't think your way into this. You can't find your voice by musing on it. You have to speak, roar, pant, moan, groan and growl. You have to let the experience guide the expression instead of the expression coming first, being a disconnected utterance lacking association with the embodied experience of pleasure (or lack thereof).

The truth of the matter is that if you're experiencing pleasure but don't feel called to make sound, you don't need to make sound. If you're getting fucked and you want to roar instead of doing sexy-girl moans and panting, you must do this for your own integrity and the full representation of your sexual journey.

And let's get this straight: if you are getting bounced about by your partner or your own hand and you feel called to go for some full-throttle sexy-girl moans and calls, then fucking do it. Whatever is real to you is right. Don't hold back.

But, many women ask, will I be judged? Will I still be loveable and worthy when I show this wild side of myself to my lover and the world?

These are questions that come up a lot. When we stretch outside the normative and begin playing in truth, fears arise around how we'll be received. The only thing you have control over is yourself. You can't determine how someone else will perceive you – and really, in this life, that is not your job. By expanding into the fullness of who you are, you set the stage for calling in a partner who is doing the same.

Your job as an elevated sex explorer is to be true to yourself: to show up with love and courage, and to be open to the fact that embodied, authentic women are a rarity in this world. By being true, you permit others to do the same.

Sure, be discerning. You don't always have to share all aspects of yourself with everyone all the time. You get to choose if the moment isn't appropriate or aligned to you sharing what it is you feel or believe. But ultimately, in the bedroom, you want to work towards full release. To be yourself, safe and alive in your own skin, able to let go and be perfect just as you are.

Sharing your truth

We know sharing your truth is a big calling, and there might be a huge journey ahead of you. We're undoing societal and cultural shame and narratives, healing our own histories and the loads we carry from our family lines, breaking through all of the imagery and representations that inundate us daily, and we're coming up against the contract of our own identity: who we think we are versus the truth of the full, whole, epic human that's within, waiting to be unleashed.

For us, this is the path we'll walk for a lifetime.

We don't do it to try to be better. It's not a feeling of seeking or trying to find. Instead, it's an intention and desire to be truthful, lit up and present, and this intention leads the way to the shedding of layers and, ultimately, to deep, soulful discoveries as the years of this life unfold.

You are so worthy of pleasure. In your fullest expression, you are perfect. Even if you've never heard someone roar like you, or seen someone get a fully blissed-out, slack-jawed facial expression paired with staccato gasps and moans, it's all welcome if you choose to love it all and follow this path of elevated sex.

Sure, you might have to have a conversation with your lover that goes a little something like: 'FYI, I'm exploring being totally free during sex. I might make noises or expressions that seem weird. They only seem weird, though, because we've all been conditioned to believe expressive sexuality looks and sounds a certain way. We can chat about it if you like. I just wanted you to know that my intention is to be free and true and let go entirely. How does that sound to you?' To us, this sounds like a refreshing, confident and exciting statement, and it allows space for your partner to step up, too.

Game: 'Here's what I like, what about you?'

Take turns with your partner sharing and affirming your sexual likes. See if you can stay in an open, playful place where you don't take anything personally but instead create space for both you and your partner to share what lights you up.

Try sharing five things you like and five things you don't like. Go back and forth, turn for turn, starting with your likes. At the end of every sentence say, 'How about you?' You can either riff off what your partner says or say something off-piste. Let it flow. At the end of the game, close with the question, 'What do you want to do?' and both answer it.

Here's how it looks in action . . .

Partner 1: I like slow anal, how about you?

Partner 2: I like heavy petting with clothes on until I come, how about you?

Go back and forth five times, then . . .

Partner 1: I don't like being on top for too long, how about you?

Partner 2: I don't like having my bum played with unless I've just showered, how about you?

Go back and forth five times, then . . .

Partner 1: What do you want to do?

Partner 2: Make out, dry hump, then shower together. What do you want to do?

Partner 1: Play with your bum, go slow and have anal.

See if you both agree and feel excited about the quest ahead, and then dive in and give it a go. If not, find a creative compromise where both partners can get their desires met. Use communication throughout and let this be an opportunity for clear dialogue, play and learning about yourself and one another.

Often, the simplest, briefest, most clear conversations are the most difficult to have because we're not used to being so clear and so self-possessed. But this is your life. What else are you going to do? Show up in half-truths, holding back what wants to come through you? If you do this in the bedroom, this way of being will unfold in all other aspects of your life – your creative output, your work, your parenting, all other relationships. And relationships and community are what we are all about as humans.

This intimate space of sexual discovery, expressed alone or with a lover, is a fertile garden for who you are and how you show up. Use it as such. Let it illuminate your voice and your expression so you can finally be free to speak your truth – and moan, grunt and wail your pleasure sounds, however they arise in your body.

How to talk about sex, distilled

- Communication is key to elevated sex, and requires knowing yourself so that you speak and move from your heart, letting your ego and need to be right fall by the wayside.
- Co-listening and holding space will give you the practice you need to truly listen and witness your partner while becoming more adept at expressing your truth.
- Take responsibility for yourself instead of projecting on to your partner. This strengthens your relationship and assists you in becoming clearer on where you have agency so you can make changes in yourself instead of passing the buck on to your lover.
- When you free your voice and find your own pleasure noises and sexual vocabulary, a sense of empowerment permeates not only your lovemaking but every facet of life.
- Don't be afraid to lighten up, play a game and learn about yourself and your partner by introducing new tools to learn and grow through fun.

6

Your body

The body is a temple to pleasure and ecstasy, and yet most people are having the kind of sex that barely registers on the Richter scale of true, warm and juicy goodness, let alone achieving its full orgasmic potential. Why is this? Why, if the body has such an expansive magnitude for receiving and offering pleasure, is this experience of pleasure not coming alive for so many people?

To be honest, we're not up on the science of pleasure and how the brain works. We were tempted to offer you some background on neurotransmitters and dopamine, but the truth is, that's just not our area of expertise. What we do know about are the energetics of pleasure – or moreover, what seems to be happening in this day and age when it comes to living in pleasure, feeling pleasure in the body and allowing pleasure to truly inhabit our every cell and lead us through life.

So what exactly is pleasure when it comes to the embodied experience?

Pleasure is a sensory experience. It belongs to the senses. It's a phenomenon that's felt in and of the body and is reliant on our ability and capacity to feel. Pleasure is about feeling good. It's about enjoyment, arousal, turn-on. It's not inherently sexual, but it is inherently sensual.

Sensual means belonging to the senses. It's when the physical body is gratified, satisfied and brought online, into full receptivity. It's when your senses – sight, sound, taste, touch, smell – are ignited and your body's receptors register the experience as good – really good.

Pleasure is initiated through the sensory body (although thinking can also bring pleasure online in the body), so it's more apt to say that it's experienced through the body, sometimes activated through the body and sometimes via the mind as the entry point.

The issue in our day and age, especially when it comes to receiving limitless pleasure in sex, is that many people aren't connected to pleasure at all. They're living fast-paced lives, disconnected from their bodies and from their sensual desires – and from the fulfilment of said desires – so that when it comes to sex and intimacy, their bodies simply aren't open and available to the expansive unfolding of pleasure that comes when an individual is connected and alive in their flesh and bones.

You might be thinking that this doesn't entirely make sense. More than ever, people are living lives fuelled by the fulfilment of their desires – drinking, eating, fucking and consuming their way through life. This carnal expression must be indicative of pleasure, right?

Not necessarily. In our experience, we've witnessed and walked the path of disembodied pleasure, looking to fill a void by consuming, instead of coming into wholeness by connecting to the entirety of ourselves. Just because you're fucking and drinking and living it up, doesn't mean you're in connection with your body and your body's ability to receive and express pleasure.

When a person is seeking to fill a void and doing so from a disembodied space, their feeling self is barely present. The mind encourages the doing from a place of longing and fear, while the body isn't attended to or fully engaged, meaning it can't actually experience what it is that's transpiring. In these cases, the body is being bypassed. Even though the activities are of the body, the body and the individual's capacity for true pleasure are not the focal point or the primary reason for engaging in said activities.

So now we get to the *why*: why in the hell are people living this way? Why are we consuming like hungry ghosts – media, food, booze, technology, coffee, meds, cigarettes, anything we can – living in our bodies while totally disconnected from them, and feeling unfulfilled emotionally, physically, sexually and spiritually?

Pace has something to do with it. Of course, it's not the entire issue, but let's go down the rabbit hole slowly to see some of the layers before we tackle what's going on down in the mossy depths.

Exploring pleasure

Being on the receiving end of pleasure requires presence. Presence requires being here now. Most of us are not here now. In fact, we're everywhere else but here.

We're in our heads, focusing on our worries, wants and concerns. We're in the past, trying to work through some previous situation. We're in the future, trying to sort out what might happen. We're mired by the way we perceive ourselves, wondering if others see us in the same way. We're mired by the way we imagine others perceive us, afraid to take a misstep and get it all wrong. (And what is a misstep, anyway? Our educational systems have us all believing that making a mistake is something to avoid at all costs instead of an opportunity to learn and grow – but that's another story.)

We're not here, living in the fullness of this physical body, because we've decided to take up residence in our mind-spaces, living like bobbleheads with an overinflated relationship to our brains and a shrivelled relationship to the rest of the flesh suit.

We know, this sounds extreme. You might be thinking, 'Wow, this Lacey and Flynn couple are rather dramatic at times, aren't they?' But seriously, reflect on it. How much time do you spend thinking about things compared to how much time you spend actually feeling your life?

You see willowy clouds drifting across a rich, blue sky. You think, 'That's lovely,' but what do you feel?

You scarf down a dinner-time burrito. You think, 'This is yum,' but what do you truly taste?

You smell a fragrance in the air. You think, 'Is that jasmine?' but do you pause and inhale again and again, filling your body, just for joy, with the intoxicating aroma?

You pass someone playing music on the street. You think, 'I love this song,' but do you stop to listen, to fully listen, and enjoy the music filling your ears?

Your lips touch your lover's in the morning. You say, 'Have a great day babe,' but did you even feel their lips, the softness, the wet, the warmth? Were you fully there to receive what was available in that very moment? Or were you already planning your to-do list for the day?

Being in our heads not only disembodies us, but also promotes a pace of life that's not sensual or sustainable. Our thoughts can run a mile a minute, faster than any other aspect of self. The sensual body does not live on that clock, but that clock – dominated by productivity, self-doubt and criticism, and planning instead of experiencing – has taken over.

The 'sixth sense' isn't our capacity to think and, as a result, live a rapid-fire life. In fact, the sixth sense is usually defined as a capacity for *knowing* things, deep down, on an intuitive or clairvoyant level. This has nothing to do with the mind and everything to do with an authentic connection to the inner realms. What we're saying is that your mind isn't a sense. It's awesome and powerful and all that stuff, and it can stimulate pleasure, sure, but it doesn't *receive* it. Your body does.

In order to enjoy the senses – to enjoy your body – you must go at a pace that envelops and invites the senses into the core of your life. This is a slower pace than the one at which most of us are going. In order to experience the full scope of pleasure, then, in life and in sex, maybe we all need to slow down a bit. Maybe we need to value going slow a whole lot more.

This doesn't mean living like a sweet and gooey snail, pulling yourself along the garden path, or just having sex like Patrick and Demi, *Ghost*-style. It means letting the pace of your life and thoughts settle so that you can bring your body back online and actually feel what in the hell is happening to you, for you and around you.

As we drop a little further down the rabbit hole, let's look at feeling – properly feeling our feelings – and how this shapes our ability to receive pleasure.

Feel your feelings

When we live fast and don't feel, where do the feelings go?

When you get sad but you don't express it, cry, share it, release it, process it, where does that sadness go? Does it just disappear because you suppressed it and willed it to go away?

The answer is, unfortunately not. Unprocessed emotions linger in the body. We know this experientially, because we've enquired within, looked at our own embodied journeys, done the work and come out the other side.

When you feel something but don't *feel it*, it doesn't just evaporate into the ether. It usually goes underground, into the subterranean creases and crevices of the body, waiting to be felt and released so your being can be cleansed of the experience.

When we become accustomed to *not* feeling, the body's capacity for holding these feelings expands – but at the same time, our capacity for living in numbness also expands. You can feel certain frequencies of life, but the depth, the magnitude, the nuance, all get lost.

This happens with trauma. Trauma is when we've experienced something distressing and this event hasn't been emotionally and spiritually healed and integrated. It's what lingers after we've been through something and we didn't heal on the emotional, energetic and spiritual plane.

There are different types of trauma, and many different teachings that will probably benefit you. This is a worthwhile pursuit in understanding yourself if you feel that trauma is impacting you. Truth be told, trauma is probably impacting all of us.

From schoolyard antics that shaped us in unpleasant ways, to abuse – sexual, physical and emotional – to physical accidents where we didn't process our experience, trauma isn't reserved for a chosen few. We're probably all traumatised, and this is both disheartening and helpful to understand.

For this journey towards elevated sex, unpacking your trauma is going to be important. Talking about what happened is a great start. As we have already said, this is best done first in person with an attuned professional. To get to the next layer of healing and integration, the body needs to be involved, tended to, moved from within and expressed to fully process and release the signature of trauma. Keep this in mind as you venture down your path.

After you've had some in-person help, entering into a process like the one we're sharing can be both helpful and fruitful instead of being, well, traumatising. We don't want to make things worse; we want to make things better. There's no prize for diving in at the deep end when you can't swim.

Fear

So, we've got unprocessed feelings, we've got trauma, we've got the pace of our lives. And what else do we have in the rabbit hole of 'Oh my god, where has the pleasure gone?'

It's more than likely that at the bottom, as is the case with almost everything that's holding us back in life, we've got the big old F-bomb: fear.

Not willing to be vulnerable and let yourself be seen? Feel uncomfortable getting naked and doing that animalistic position you've been dreaming of? Choosing relentlessly to focus on the to-do list rather than getting wet, hard and wild? It's probable that the reason you're saying no to pleasure, or the potential for pleasure, is because you're scared.

You're scared of feeling what has to be felt before pleasure can be activated subtly or fully in your body. You've spent so long not feeling that when you tap in to the space, too much of what wants to arise is very scary, so it seems better to keep a lid on it. You're scared of slowing down, letting go, letting in and being here now, because how can you get shit done if you drop in and let go? You're afraid of feeling into the depths of your heart, allowing the pleasure on the surface of your skin to move into joy – and, ultimately, love –because what happens if you get hurt? So instead, you stick with the carnal satisfaction and never let the rolling pleasure pierce your soul.

And what about this doozy: you're afraid of the rapture of pleasure and of being overcome by enjoyment of your body. You're afraid – without knowing it on a conscious level and therefore choosing it intentionally – of being so thrust into feeling that you forget to think, that your contract with yourself and this world of who you purport to be and how you do things dissolves, until all that's left is euphoria and the potential for accepting that this life isn't about suffering after all, but is instead about immense joy and boundless love – and you, dear one, are front and centre.

Why in the hell would anyone be afraid of that amount of goodness? Why would we spend our lives avoiding exactly what we all proclaim to want the most?

Herein lies the rub, the sweetest and simplest trick: the exact thing we want is available to us in any given moment, but we have to be brave enough to stop searching and start being. We have to intend on healing and then let healing in. We must stop doing and start being here for the experience of life. We need to allow the flow instead of forcing the dam. This truly is an invitation into the realm of the feminine for us all. But because we've lived lives in the masculine – and not the authentic masculine, but the distorted – we've lost touch with how to be, how to heal, how to embody and stop doing. We've lost touch with ourselves.

And now, it's time to come home.

Self-love

Let's talk self-love, a cliché forged in the meme fires of social media. It seems that everything worthwhile gets twisted into a farce at some point, so let's dust this baby off and plant it in the centre of our hearts, shall we?

Listen, you probably have an up-and-down relationship with old numero uno: yourself. You're hard on yourself, your self-talk is a tad on the aggro side, to say the least, and inside your mind-space, you're just a bit of an ass to yourself.

But this is going to have to change, at least incrementally, if you're going to open up to boundless pleasure, orgasmic bliss and a life of elevated sex. When we say it like that, what kind of person is going to say no? We'll tell you who. The person who says, 'It's good for some, isn't it?' The person who hears this and thinks, 'That's just not for me. It sounds good, but that kind of bliss is for unicorn humans, and not regular everyday Josephines and Joes.'

Have you done that yourself – discredited yourself and your ability to have what you want, to live in pleasure, to have epic sex and the whole nine yards? Because if you've already decided that this isn't for you, then it won't be for you.

In order to make this a reality, you have to love your sweet self enough to let the possibility of pleasure into your heart. And when you do let it into your heart, you'll probably find it was actually there the whole time, waiting to be activated and unleashed.

Self-love, awakening love in yourself for yourself, is an imperative part of coming into the fullness of yourself, and ultimately giving and receiving love from someone else.

Your self-image has everything to do with this. Who do you perceive yourself to be? And what do you believe to be true about your body? If you hate yourself and your body, you probably won't be able to receive the full expanse of love, adoration and pleasure available to you. Instead, you'll be blocking it with your own beliefs about yourself and how you're not worthy of receiving it. It's amazing how our beliefs, the thoughts we have about who we are, can actually impact the physical body's ability to receive and open up to pleasure.

So, it's time to love yourself. It's time to love your body. And no, this usually isn't done in one fell swoop, unless you have a monumental awakening that quantum-leaps your healing process. We're here for it all – the long road and the swift path of awakening to your mega-epic, radiant power. For most of us, this is a journey: one that you might as well start right now.

Tools to help on the path of self-love

Of course, we're going to come at this from a non-traditional self-love vantage point. Rock your affirmations, rock your meditations, and let's spice things up with some elevated sex tools.

Naming your bits

We talked about this in the previous chapter, and now we want to make sure this has been anchored in. If you avoided this, well, the joke's on you, because we're hound dogs and we're not going to let up until you've truly sunk your teeth in and explored the language you use for your genitals.

So, what's it going to be?

Pussy? Cock? Cunt? Dick?

We're not fussy. We just want you to have fun. And yet by this, we mean moving beyond the juvenile space of making fun of things, and into the adult space of power and maturity. It's about choosing words that you can work with to feel more connected and confident when speaking about your sexual body (to yourself or someone else).

Pussy Gazing

Lacey began teaching the practice of Pussy Gazing (much to our surprise and the surprise of many others) in 2018. After seeing how powerful the practice was when prepping for the birth of our first baby, she realised she couldn't keep it to herself, and so set up her first workshop in east London in a lofty warehouse studio.

LACEY

When the urge came to me to create this workshop, I was like, hell no! I felt both delighted by the idea and mortified. Could I really offer a workshop where women came to look at their vulvas alongside other women? And furthermore, who in the hell would come to such a wacky event? The answers are: I definitely could do it, and many women would come. When I sold my first ticket to that first event, I was just happy I wouldn't be alone. I actually thought, 'That's great, there will be two of us.' But then the workshop sold out, and we were about fifteen women with mirrors, getting up close and personal with our bodies in what many would say, in the end, felt oddly normal, even if they were quite unsure or nervous to start with.

Here's some of the feedback:

'How exciting to feel liberated looking at my vagina. Something I never thought I'd find myself doing. Very empowering.'

'I saw pain, shame and hate drifting away with ease and grace.'

'I learned that I was holding a lot of shame and sadness in me. I'm ready to heal now.'

'I felt incredibly at ease, weirdly normal and relaxed. This practice reminds me how to receive, surrender and soften into my full-spectrum femininity.'

'What I saw was truly beautiful. How had I ignored her power for so long?'

'This workshop made me see my body and my sexual self in a very different way. I realised I was carrying around an unbelievable amount of shame and embarrassment when it came to sex. I feel more available and open to expressing what I want now.'

Lacey went on to teach this workshop in London and Berlin, selling out every time, sometimes with fewer mirrors than pussies (which was her favourite problem to have). She also taught it online for other companies and events, as well as at festivals, and even had her workshops featured in the press and on TV. Needless to say, there was a desire for it, and many women were ready to stretch outside their comfort zones in order to heal and thrive.

So, how in the heck is this practice done?

Well, yes, it is very much what it says on the tin: you get a mirror and you look at your vulva. But it's much more than a cursory glance or peek. This is the art of sustained looking – of moving from judgement and appraisal to lovingly gazing – so that discovery, healing and expansion can take place.

Here are some tips for creating your own Pussy Gazing journey. To get a fully guided video version of this practice, hop over to our website at laceyandflynn.com.

What you'll need:

- a quiet space where you feel free to be naked with yourself, where no one will interrupt you, and you can truly unwind and be present
- a good-sized hand mirror (a compact is too small, although at one festival, where around seventy-five women attended, many did use compacts as Lacey ran out of proper mirrors)
- objects to create the space: gentle music, candles, incense (these are optional, but nice extras if you'd like to make it more of a ritual)
- a journal/notebook/paper and pen

Tips for Pussy Gazing

Women have asked Lacey over the years: 'Why would I go to an event or be guided to do this when I can do it by myself?' Of course, you can rock this practice solo. Like any embodied journey – yoga, ecstatic dance, meditative movement – you can do it alone or in a group. The benefit of the group or being guided is that you are supported; you can get out of your own head about it, and you can drop in deeper because of the space that's created.

Nonetheless, there is power in a home practice, so let's get to it.

- First things first, take some time to drop in to your body. You can dance to a few songs, give yourself a solo massage, meditate, do some gentle and slow stretching – basically, the intention is to begin grounding yourself, quieting the mind and getting present.
- You can be clothed, in a flowing robe or naked for this entire journey – it's up to you. When Lacey does it in a group, usually everyone is wearing a skirt and has a blanket handy if they get chilly.
- Once you've arrived, and have started to unwind and drop in to the space, take some time to just be and breathe, setting an intention for the journey. What do you want to feel or experience? For example: 'My intention is to heal shame and connect more fully with myself,' or, 'My intention is to find beauty and love myself.' Anything that feels aligned and powerful for you.
- The next step (and keep in mind, for the sake of simplicity, this is a pared-back version of the journey) is to place your hands lovingly between your legs, noticing what comes up. Shame? Resistance to touching yourself in this way? Fear of being caught or found out? Numbness? Whatever it is, allow it, welcome it all in and greet your experience with love and tenderness.
- Without rushing, it's time for gazing. Hold your mirror and take a moment to look at your face and into

your own eyes. Remind yourself of your intention and
find love for yourself and this moment. Slowly scan
the mirror down your body until it lands between
your legs.

- You can be sitting up at this stage, propped up with
  pillows – any posture where you can get a good look.
- Once here, get comfortable and commence
  gazing. Soften your eyes and jaw, and simply look.
  Maintain the energy of an easeful stare and notice
  what arises – judgement on the way you look, past
  memories, feelings of discomfort. It's all welcome.
- The task now is to stay: to simply be here now and
  to maintain the practice for a while. Just like with
  meditation, the longer you stay, the deeper you
  cascade into yourself.
- Feel free to use your hands to part your labia if you
  want a fuller look. At first, you might be more curious,
  looking with a detective's gaze, as it's likely you've
  never looked at yourself in this way before.
- Eventually, find stillness and a soft gaze, repeating
  your intention whenever you need to anchor back in.
- Try staying for fifteen to twenty minutes – longer
  if you're able. Let the layers of the journey reveal
  themselves. Whatever happens is perfect and has the
  chance to teach you something.
- If the desire for self-touch arises, greet it. But do it
  without a destination. This is not about a quick fix,
  rubbing one out. This is about awakening and true
  connection.
- When you're done, take your time to breathe, set
  aside your mirror and find gratitude for the practice.

- You can end the way you began, with some movement, breathing or self-touch if you like.
- Once you've wrapped the embodied aspect of the journey, take some time to journal on the experience: What did you see? What did you feel? What did you learn? What surprised you?

Feel free to come back to this practice. Lacey did it again and again every single day while she was preparing for her first freebirth. She credits the practice with helping her heal her relationship to her body and sexuality, creating the terrain for a powerful and enjoyable birth, and also igniting her self turn-on, ultimately healing her relationship to Flynn. If she can do it, so can you.

Cock Gazing

There's a stigma around men doing these kinds of practices. When women do it, it's hot and spiritual, but when men do it, it's perverted and a bit dodgy. But why? Why is it that masculinity has been so distorted that a man looking at or enjoying his body outside sex or the realm of porn is weird?

Think about it. However you identify, reflect now on your own views of what makes a man powerful when it comes to sex? Most people don't conjure up an image of a man, staring at his own cock in a full-length mirror, turning himself on. But if you've ever seen an empowered man doing this – or been one yourself – it's a beautiful thing.

With that, let's get to it.

Cock Gazing is a bit different from Pussy Gazing. Flynn hasn't taught this in a group setting, but it's something he's done himself as part of his elevated sex journey, and something he's shared with his one-to-one clients.

This practice is most powerfully done in front of a full-length mirror. It's an integration practice that encompasses gazing, some touch and a calling in of the integrated and healed masculine. No big deal, right?

What you'll need:

- just like with Pussy Gazing, a quiet and private space where you feel free to be naked with yourself, where no one will interrupt you and you can truly unwind and be present
- a full-length mirror: floor to ceiling is preferred, but basically, just use the biggest mirror you have in your house so you can see as much of your body as possible
- objects to create the space: you might enjoy some music, candles, incense, anything that beautifies and creates a ritualistic experience
- a journal and pen

Tips for Cock Gazing

- Get set up in front of the mirror. You can be fully clothed to begin with.

- At first, take some time to drop in to yourself. Do some deep breathing, movement, big exhalations or grunts and gorilla chest-bumps to get into this place, in your body, in this exact moment in time. Do what feels good in the moment.
- Once you drop in to yourself, you can begin to undress. Take your time, feel your clothes on your body, and allow yourself to be in a mindful space (body-ful is more like it, as we don't want you in your mind – that word can be a bit confusing!).
- This might bring up some discomfort around what a man looks and feels like when he's undressing. Masculine sensuality is an underdeveloped and under-expressed area, misrepresented in media and porn. This gives men no blueprint or gauge on what other embodied, sensual and powerful men are doing, so you're going to have to be brave here as you navigate this new terrain.
- Once you're naked, take yourself in. Often, the first layer is judgement and appraisal – perhaps saying nasty things in your mind about your precious body. You don't need to change what's happening, but take note. Take note of how this inner dialogue makes you feel, what comes up and the energy surrounding it all.
- Now, step closer to the mirror and look at your own eyes. If you've eye gazed before, that's what you're doing right now, but instead of having a partner for this journey, you're rocking it solo. Settle your breathing, find steadiness in your stance and simply look at yourself.

- Notice what comes up. If you have a desire to stop, don't. Stick with it.
- Set an intention for your time: to connect with yourself, to become a more present man and lover, to heal how you perceive your body, to feel more powerful and alive – whatever motivates and inspires you is perfect.
- After a couple of minutes of softly looking at your own eyes, take your hands and place them on your cock. You're probably not used to simply holding your body in this way. This isn't about bravado or jerking off. This is an intentional holding, bringing you into connection with your cock-space.
- Keep softening in your body and breathing, then let your eyes settle on your hands and cock.
- Let your hands fall away now as you take in your cock-space, noticing what comes up as you come into connection with this part of your body and being.
- Let the first layer of judgement and appraisal arise, and stay here, breathing, until you drop in to the next layer – a more meditative space.
- Perhaps your hands want to find your cock, holding and touching in curiosity and exploration. This isn't a wank session, fellas. This is about connection, first with the eyes and then with the hands, making a circuit of tactility and witnessing.
- Naturally, because many cocks love to get erect, it makes sense to explore this here, with this new intention. Again, this isn't masturbation, but a chance to be erect and witness the full splendour of your

cock. You might like to start massaging from the base of your shaft to the tip.

- Tap in to what comes up for you. Do you feel comfortable in your skin? Does this feel like a waste of time? Challenge yourself to stay in this space a few minutes longer.
- When you're ready to wind down, take your time to breathe. Come back to the full view of yourself and feel gratitude for this practice.
- Once you've wrapped the embodied aspect of this journey, take some time to journal on your experience. What did you see? What did you feel? What did you learn? What surprised you?
- Can you imagine where you'd be in your body if you did this practice once a week? Or once a day when you get out of the shower?

Now, this might make you uncomfortable to read, let alone do, but if you're devoted to the path of elevated sex, to coming into yourself and giving and receiving pleasure to your maximum capacity, then you're going to be willing to show up and do things like this, no matter how weird they sound (or feel).

One of the biggest parts of the Cock Gazing journey is letting yourself be in relative stillness and presence. There's nothing to do, there's nothing to achieve and there's no quick orgasm to reach. In fact, this is 100 per cent *not* about orgasm. Dropping your goal mentality as the masculine is imperative to coming into presence for this practice.

It's likely that you have a lifetime of judgements to release around your penis: its size and shape, what that means about you as a man. If you were circumcised (like Flynn), then you probably have this normalised trauma lingering in your body. There's actually a lot going on when it comes to your penis, and so this practice is important if you want to acknowledge and heal anything that's holding you back in your body and in your power.

We've found that this set-up works better for dudes than the hand mirror used in Pussy Gazing, both for physiological reasons and also on the energetic level. Men are often much more comfortable masturbating, and so lying back and having a wank is no biggie. But placing a man upright, faced with his own gaze, in a state of appraising and then softening into witnessing himself, is new terrain.

Why self-pleasure?

Self-pleasure is the process of making love to yourself. This isn't masturbation – having a quick wank, rubbing one out, flogging the dolphin, spanking the monkey, or whatever other animal abuse innuendos can be mustered up for touching your own genitals. Instead, this is a journey of deeper connection. What did you expect from us – a sixty-second vibrator session for the sake of climax?

Let's get this straight: we both love a good orgasm. But in our goal-orientated society, where everything is geared towards an end result as a metric for success, orgasm has become a little too all-encompassing (and, truthfully, quite stressful for many people).

We'll talk about this more in chapter nine, which will get into the nitty-gritty of prioritising the journey over the destination, but for now, please know you don't get a gold star for cumming.

The self-pleasure manifesto

When it comes to touching yourself, there's probably a lot going on beyond the act at hand. Remember when we said everything has a story? With self-pleasure, there are probably loads of the storylines you addressed in chapter four, which might include shame, dissociation, disembodiment and unprocessed trauma, amongst other heavy-hitters.

You're probably not accustomed to touching yourself for very long either, making self-pleasure different to a quick wank. You don't need to sign up for some lengthy ordeal, but this certainly isn't about satisfying the itch of release. Instead, this is about truly getting to know your body – what you like, what turns you on – and being the initiator and receiver of magnitudes of pleasure and all your own love.

You might be squirming just reading this, thinking it's not for you, but self-pleasure is for every single person with a pulse. You see, activating your own pleasure potential and becoming empowered to be the leader of your body in the realm of sex is the mark of an elevated sex practitioner.

And, to make it even more basic, having shame around touching your own body is a devastating result of religion, social conditioning and myriad other structures that have duped you into believing your own body is inherently wrong and touching it is sinful.

We must, for the sake of ourselves and the future of our species, heal these ridiculous ideas. In fact, they're more than ideas, aren't they? They're internalised structures that we all uphold through believing them and then acting upon their instruction.

There is nothing in nature that teaches us that our bodies are wrong, or that we're wrong for having these bodies or enjoying them. If you turn to nature for the answer, she tells us to live, bloom and thrive. She teaches us not to dim our expression for fear of outshining another. There is no blueprint in this world (besides the constructs our species have fabricated and upheld) to connect shame with pleasure, nor with self-pleasure.

Self-pleasure vs masturbation

Self-pleasure is the act of inducing pleasure in your own body. It is being the conduit and cause for your own joy and satisfaction. It is activating your own sexual desire or, at the very least, fulfilling the promise of sexual, perhaps orgasmic, potential in your own luscious form.

And to make it really simple: self-pleasure is touching your own genitals and enjoying it.

That being said, self-pleasure isn't always pleasurable. Sometimes on the journey of touching yourself, you discover things that aren't pleasurable. It's not uncommon to experience shame, fear, numbness or a disconnect on this journey. If there's stuff to work through on the corporeal level, these things might come up too, such as unprocessed anger, sadness or frustration. Self-pleasure can be a pathway into healing fresh and calcified emotions that need expressing and releasing.

So, we have a perception of self-pleasure that might dissuade us, which is based on the way we were raised, our parents' views, religion, culture, etc. And then we have our own embodied experiences (such as trauma and disconnect) to contend with as we navigate bringing this new practice into our lives.

Maybe you use the word 'masturbation'. It's a bit mechanical for our liking, associated with schoolroom discussions of wet dreams and puberty. You might like to dust it off and power-language that shit, but we've opted for self-pleasure – two words that offer a promise of the journey ahead.

Let's actually choose to differentiate masturbation from self-pleasure, because they have two very different intentions. (As we said above, you can still use 'masturbation' if 'self-pleasure' feels too 'ooh-la-la' for you, but let's imbue it with the energy required to make this the process as it's intended to be.)

Masturbation is goal-orientated. Not many people do it without the intention of having an orgasm.

Self-pleasure, on the other hand, is the path of pleasure without a goal. You might naturally orgasm as a result of the path of pleasure, but you're not trying to get off in order to feel optimal or fully satisfied.

Self-pleasure is a practice while masturbation is a means to an end.

Self-pleasure for men and women

Let's start with women

Self-pleasure is taboo for women.

Even though we're in a time where body-positivity and self-love have been anchored into the public psyche as worthwhile frameworks by which to live, touching oneself is still not something most people are shouting about at parades (or writing on affirmation posters – we've yet to see 'Live, Love, Laugh, Masturbate' home decor at a holiday beach rental, for example.)

There's a deep-seated shame for women around 'wanting it' and having desire. Because these inclinations have been associated with sluttiness, women walk a fine line when it comes to claiming their sexuality. Even though there's now freedom like never before with proclaiming one's own sexual expression, we still find in our work that most women carry shame around touching themselves, even if they do it regularly.

It's fascinating, isn't it? To do something and enjoy it, something for one's own body alone, and to feel bad about it.

We don't need to unpack all the issues around feminine sexual expression right now (we'll do that in the next chapter), but we will say that everyone reading this is not alone in their trepidation around the topic. And because many women have an icky feeling that their vulvas are weird, ugly, too hairy, smelly, creamy, etc., a distance has developed between selfhood and the pussy.

Women are often afraid to touch themselves with any level of confidence.

6

LACEY

I often guide my students to do a practice where they simply cup their pussy region. They do this clothed, with both hands. Even when they're doing it solo at home, over an online session where nobody can see them, they still attest to feeling awkward and like they're doing something wrong. Think about this (like, really muse on it): a woman alone at home, fully clothed, cupping her pussy, feels like she shouldn't be doing what she's doing. That's some deep conditioning right there, isn't it?

If you're in that boat, you're so not alone. This is a very common experience, and thus it can be very difficult to develop a self-pleasure practice.

Even my one-to-one premium clients, who are paying me to learn this stuff, still resist doing the practices, because the resistance can be so strong after living for decades with shame around touching our bodies in this way.

———————————————— , ————————————————

It's easy to brush this off and feel like we're talking to someone else and not you. But we're not talking to someone else: we're talking directly to you. Yes, you!

All women have the right to enjoy their own bodies if they so desire. And if they don't so desire, then that's another powerful thing to investigate.

And now for the men

Men have been used to projecting their desire outwards, feeling what feels good through the lens of being turned on by the other: watching porn or creating mental fantasies, for example.

Most men aren't used to being turned on in and of themselves. This is similar for women, but it has a different flavour for men. The men we work with watch porn far more frequently than their female counterparts do (most of the women aren't watching at all, actually). A distinction we've come to is that men don't feel comfortable being their own source of pleasure.

They'll watch something or think about something, and this feels safe and normal, but when instructed to touch themselves and *feel* it, there's awkwardness and almost a sense of being lost. Some men fantasise during sex with their partner every time they have sex. They think about other women, instead of what they're doing in the moment and draw on scenes from porn in order to coax turn-on into their bodies. The body's sensory faculties aren't enough, because they're not accustomed to fully feeling, dropping in and being present.

For men, it's normal and expected that they masturbate, because male sexuality is seen as hungry and needing a quick fix. The topic isn't overly discussed, though, save for in jest. The idea of authentic self-touch for men is almost too intimate to fathom for most, so it gets reduced to a joke about horniness and insatiability.

Men are expected to be desirous and fulfil this desire by consuming. When there's nothing to consume to sate the desire, shame and fear will almost certainly arise. You might ask yourself: 'What does this mean about me as a man if I pleasure myself for the enjoyment of the journey and not for the purpose of an orgasm?'

But as you can tell, men who are open and ready for it have extraordinary breakthroughs when they move beyond porn and fantasies into the embodied landscape and feeling of their bodies, experiencing instead of witnessing or thinking to stimulate the felt sense.

We've seen in men that their psyches start to change. They start to connect with a deeper level of pleasure in and of themselves. They tap in to a new level of joy and fulfilment in their lives as a whole, creating a feeling of expansion, depth and lightness: something we're sure we can all agree men can use more of.

How to self-pleasure for men and women

Here are a few simple things to keep in mind (and in pussy and cock) when you're getting down to it:

1. This isn't about orgasm; this is about discovering what feels good, and not just doing the thing you know will make you cum.
2. Set aside some time and take it seriously. We know, taking touching yourself seriously might seem weird, but this is a pretty big reframe and reclamation, so give it the time and space it deserves.
3. Try touching yourself in ways you wouldn't normally (slow, gentle strokes around the genitals and across your whole body; wide, open palms; petting, swirling, tapping, gently tugging). Again, this is learning a new language beyond the quick-fire cum.
4. Notice what arises in your body as you unfold the practice. When you meet shame, resistance or anything that says you're bad or wrong, instead of pushing it away, breathe into it. Often, we want to cram down the yucky stuff to make it go away. Instead, try to give it space to fully articulate without identifying with it. Once you give it space, it will probably soften and perhaps even dissipate.
5. Feel free to set a timer so that you engage with the practice for twenty minutes or so, and then continue your journey within this framework. During masturbation, most people orgasm then stop, but perhaps you won't orgasm, so creating structure can be helpful.
6. Take yourself to the edge and back away. Don't

hit all your hot spots right off the bat. Really play and explore. If things get cummy, slow it down and change tack. Change your breath and the focus on where you're feeling pleasure.

7. Don't bypass your turn-on. It can be easy with the process of masturbation to do what gets you off. With self-pleasure we want you to tap deeply into *arousal*. We want you to allow the natural upwelling of turn-on in your body. Go slow. Let it unfold. This is no time to rush.

Love yourself

The truth is, we all have some degree of body dissatisfaction, shame and uncertainty, and this is very true when it comes to the way we view our sexual bodies (our willies, fannies, cocks, pussies, boobs, testes and buttholes) – but the concept of body love rarely gets any airtime.

In exploring naming your bits, gazing upon them and giving yourself new degrees of pleasure, we hope a new level of confidence has been born in you. Because, ultimately, you deserve to live a life free of the shackles of shame, and with full reverence, respect and love for all aspects of yourself.

Your sexual expression is your creative and pleasure expression – and neither creativity nor pleasure are optional or frivolous. Creativity is the route to our existence, and pleasure is the joy of this life: feeling wonderful experiences in our bodies and relishing the delight of this physical form.

A liberated and expanded life is one where we elevate sex and remember neither our bodies nor our pleasure are shameful. A liberated and expanded life is one where we talk freely about the epic self-pleasure session we had around the office water cooler, without feel like perverts for it, because we're no longer uninitiated and immature, and are now fully embodied, sovereign and healed beings sharing our joy with the world. Okay, maybe the office water cooler is too far, but we can dream, can't we? What a vision for what could be if we each attend to ourselves. Let's make it happen together, one spiritual wank at a time.

'The invitation to explore self-pleasure sent profound ripples through my life. By setting aside time for this practice, just me in my body – no porn, no fantasy, no imagination – I discovered that which I'd subconsciously and subtly been seeking from relationships outside myself. Through this practice, I found tenderness, curious play, appreciation, strength, control, grace, raw emotion, stimulation, surrender, cosmic union, psychedelic electric explosion and deep rest.'

Charlie (30)

Your body, distilled

- Loving yourself is the key to loving someone else and having a profound relationship and elevated sex life.
- Pussy Gazing and Cock Gazing will help you heal shame associated with your sexual body, giving you a deeper understanding of yourself as a sexual being.
- Self-pleasure is a powerful practice for going deeper into self-love as it helps you learn to feel, connect with yourself and bring pleasure online in your own body without porn, fantasies or the aid of a partner.
- How you see yourself is a crucial component to the quality of your life overall, and plays a fundamental role in your sexual experiences.

7

The biggest issues for women in the bedroom

Women have been disempowered sexually for aeons. As a result, most women have little to no comprehension of what they truly desire in the bedroom. They've adopted their sexual expression from representations in the media and pornography, and this means their sexual expression has become a performance – for themselves and their partners – a facade they don't even realise they're putting on. Of course, this assertion of pandemic-scale disembodiment and performative sexual expression on the part of many women might be uncomfortable to hear, but we've seen it hundreds of times, and speak as well from personal experience.

Even when Lacey thought she was having sex from a place of empowerment, she was still disengaged, disembodied and not in tune with herself. There is no blame in this, for her or any woman. This is a part of the sexual awakening process: realising all the ways in which we've been sexually dormant, and then lovingly and fiercely doing something about it.

This chapter is going to be a game-changer for men and women alike. Women will be introduced to a new kind of sex: one where their pleasure matters, where they feel free to take up space, be wild and emotional, and finally claim sex for themselves. But first, they'll learn to become aware of themselves as sexual beings, developing skills for self-compassion and healing, and ultimately slingshotting their journeys into being sexually integrated humans.

Femininity and the feminine

What does it mean to be a sexual woman? What does sexual desire feel like for a woman? And how is it presented through the female body?

Before we answer all those achingly momentous questions, let's talk about femininity and the feminine.

Feminine is not a dirty word, and femininity is not a construct. Sure, these energies have been co-opted and turned into pastiche, used to debase women as lesser-than and to insult men who don't express their polarity in a way that's macho or readily understood by society. But at the centre of it all – before the corruption of these terms, energies and expressions – the concept of femininity was pure, unadulterated, natural and very much real.

Some gender-based theories would have us believe that femininity is entirely a construct, but we believe it's more complex than that. Sure, femininity and the feminine have become a series of tropes that sit on the surface, having more to do with appearance and behaviours – but that's only one facet of the feminine. Below the surface, there's an entire inner realm of the feminine that's mysterious, woven into the soul and womb, which makes it easy to disregard or reduce as make-believe. We've become so accustomed in our society to only believing what we can see with our eyes or what science dictates is real. And so when it comes to expressions of the feminine, we've made it skin-deep instead of soul-deep, which is the birthplace of the essences.

A journey into the feminine

Somewhere along the line, the world started hating women. There are loads of ideas on the birthplace of this distaste, depending on who you ask, but for simplicity's sake, let's all agree that ages ago, women got a bad rap. Being a woman was seen as drawing the shorter straw. Instead of both sexes sitting next to one another, celebrating their differences and honouring the unique capacities of each role, men were throned and women were ousted.

In the sixties, feminism began to dig into a range of important topics and experiences: reproductive rights, sexuality, women's place in the public sector, and the sticky space of domesticity. Women, quite rightly, wanted to be equal to men. Yet, however laudable the intention and effort, one of the unforeseen consequences was a devaluation of many of the unique characteristics and capacities of women, because many women at this time didn't want to align with certain aspects of their uniqueness. Instead, there was a push to celebrate women's likeness to men and disregard their biological differences, which makes total sense because women were often viewed as weaker simply for being women.

This was a big divorcing and disembodying point for the feminine. Sure, it had been fissuring for countless years before this, but in terms of a timeline that's close enough to grasp, we saw a real diminishing of the feminine, of biological reverence, of the beauty and power of the female form and of a woman's role, because what women represented wasn't nearly as on trend as what men did. It was a man's world and to play the game, women had to find ways to rise above their differences.

We saw menstruation become a nuisance to be solved, pregnancy as an ellipsis in a woman's life that she'd endeavour to make up for, birth as a medicalised procedure that women couldn't be trusted to undergo without the male gaze, and the total devaluation of motherhood as an imperative contribution to the fabric of a heathy society and to the emotional and spiritual wellbeing of mother and child.

Of course, feminism was important. Women deserve to be safe and free, and to govern their own lives as they see fit. This is more nuanced than that.

The way 'equality' was determined and achieved has seen the pendulum swing too far in the other direction, where women's worth is now largely based on their ability to be like men, instead of finally truly valuing what makes women epic and unique in their own right.

You might wonder what this has to do with elevated sex and women in the bedroom? We're sure you know the answer: everything.

Sex and the feminine

If sex is the dance of life, the expression that brings us all into being, if its function is procreation, joy, pleasure and healing, and a woman has no connection to herself first and foremost as a physical being, then she's going to find it challenging to tap in to the full expression of her desire, because it's all part of the same thread.

Let's put it this way: a woman who knows her body and her cycle (menstrual or overall life cycle), who understands that pregnancy, birth and the biology of her body are not shameful, and who has reckoned with her pussy and womb, is probably a sexually liberated woman. And yes, at this point in time, these women are unicorns. There aren't many of them, but that doesn't mean it's not available to us all.

'My pussy was the unknown, referred to as "down there", as something never to be spoken about. I felt embarrassment, shame and disgust with this part of myself. I have discovered, though, that my pussy is actually a source of deep pleasure, fun, joy, comfort and guidance. Lacey has shown me that Pussy is beautiful, powerful and confident, which I am now becoming too, through this new connection to myself.'

Erin (37)

Wake up your pussy

It's high time to let your pussy become a soft, supple and juicy place of awakened pleasure instead of the Saharan experience many women are facing. To wake up your pussy, you have to come to terms with her dormancy and begin a wooing process through which you become your own greatest lover, disciple and pleasure devotee.

- **Praise your pussy** Forgive yourself for all the mean things you've said and believed in the past, and begin a new narrative where you love your pussy with reckless abandon.

- **Swirl your hips and stir the honeypot** Awaken your sacral energy and begin releasing tension in your lower back, hips and pussy-space. Imagine your vulva softening and all the fleshy bits blossoming open.
- **Become intimately aware of what lights up your pussy** If you like something and it makes your pussy sing, do more of it. And do less of the shit that makes your pussy bored and sad.
- **Pat your pussy** Don't be afraid to cup, pat and draw your energy into your pussy throughout the day, waking up nerve endings and desire, and coming into your own turn-on and power.

The performance of female sexuality and desire

Owing to the chasm between a woman and her body, which severs her from her own desires, we see female sexuality as a performance-based experience for many.

Truth be told, most women have no idea what they want in the bedroom, because they haven't felt entitled to want anything. They don't know their body's sexual intricacies because they've been taught that their bodies are unimportant and problematic, and so they've become separated from their fleshy homes, ashamed of being a woman, where the least important or interesting thing about her is her biological prowess. All the extraordinary aspects of the body have been seen as pedestrian and irrelevant; something to get away from instead of something to cherish and celebrate.

As a result, we've seen female sexuality become a trope instead of an authentic lived experience. Representations in media and porn have dictated the ways in which women express themselves in the bedroom. From the positions they adopt with their bodies to the sounds they make, every aspect of sexual expression has been witnessed and then assimilated.

The issue with this is that media representations and popular conceptions around female sexuality are often one dimensional. They are not holistic or indicative of any truth or depth. These representations and conceptions are surface level, and the majority have been dictated by men, meaning they are an interpretation or a fantasy from an exterior lens. Women have not been able to dictate the perimeters of their own sexual desire or sexual expression, and because of this, we see women putting on their sexuality from the outside instead of letting it arise and be born from within.

Instead of truly feeling their bodies and expressing their innermost desires, women tend towards doing what they've seen done before. They adopt positions that aren't as pleasurable for them, because that's what they think is right; they make high-pitched pleasure sounds because that's 'more attractive' than guttural roars; and they prioritise the pleasure and enjoyment of their male counterparts instead of prioritising themselves or feeling like equals in the experience.

Deferring her pleasure

Time and time again, we see women deferring their pleasure, waiting until some future date that never comes to enjoy themselves, to feel good and to finally stand up and say, 'This is what I want, and I'm worth it.'

There's an invisible forcefield that keeps women from making such bold proclamations of desire.

From within, a woman is sure she's not allowed or worthy, and from the outside she doesn't want to be perceived as too forward or demanding. Then there's a deeper layer, which is the all-out uncertainty over what she truly wants and desires. This is born of not knowing her own body and not feeling confident and grounded in her own voice. We know, this sounds dire, but to get to the sexual ecstasy awaiting all women, we need to understand what's getting in the way first.

Ask yourself these questions:

- How can you claim what you want when you don't know what it is?
- How can you ask someone else to give you something when you don't even know what that something is?
- How can you use your voice to share and express when you don't trust yourself to speak up and claim this life?

These are huge questions and, as you see, they extend well beyond the bedroom into all parts of life.

Women haven't been given the tools to understand any of the above – nor do they even have an awareness that this isn't natural, but instead a product of being denatured – and so tend to throw their hands up when it comes to their sexuality. They'll give and receive to a certain point, but beyond that, there's a block. They have no idea how epic, satisfying, healing, expansive and spiritual sex can be, because a) they haven't been shown it, and b) they don't even know how to start with the issues at hand (or they don't recognise that these are in fact issues, and not just how it's meant to go). And so, they go along with the status quo, without knowing there's anything more.

But deep down, women *do* know. We all know. We know there's more to life than working fifty hours a week, then dying. We know there's more to relationships than running a house together, bickering, then dying. And we sure as hell know, even if it's not on a conscious level, that sex is meant to be a mutually satisfying, hot-as-hell experience that generates positive, uplifting energy, and not something that takes from either party.

True reciprocity for elevated sex

Women often feel like sex is a leeching process that's about being taken from instead of given to. It's no wonder (especially in hetero relationships) that many women can't be fucked with getting fucked, because it doesn't feel like it's truly about their needs and desires. For a woman in this situation, it's not because the person fucking her is intentionally taking from her; it's because she's disempowered, divorced from her true self and unable to take up half the space in the bedroom. So the man (who has probably initiated the whole thing to begin with) takes the space. His desire is centred, and he gets what he wants, because sex is seen as an act that's more for men than for women. The woman leaves feeling like she's given up a part of herself, albeit willingly because she wants to want sex, and she wants to connect and make him happy. In her heart and soul and pussy, she feels desaturated and taken from by the whole ordeal.

So beyond equality, and instead with harmony at heart, how can we achieve balance in the bedroom with so much to unpack and heal? How can women want sex, show up for sex, claim their desires and feel fully empowered to be sexually expressed beings – in the bedroom and out in the world? Because – let's be clear – sexual liberation is about more than an epic romp. It's about the way you carry yourself in the world, how you feel in your body, your confidence, your voice; it's about you being your whole delicious self.

Ultimately, sexual energy cannot be compartmentalised. That hasn't worked to date, has it? It's created a culture of lasciviousness, rape and aggression, sexual distortion and fear, disconnect and dissociation and sexual apathy, and made people feel ashamed for being sexual beings in the first place. If we're ashamed about the act that created us, what does that say about who we are and our capacity for thriving?

We can't thrive as a species until we're liberated from the shackles of sexual shame and repression. And we can't heal until we wake up to the fact that there's a huge problem. So, here we are: waking up together.

How to support your partner's thriving in the bedroom (and in your relationship as a whole)

As you take full control of your own sexual expression as a woman, it's imperative to understand the ways in which your actions and habitual ways of being impact your partner. Here are a few tips to support your lover as you expand into more love and connection, in yourself and in the relationship:

• Keep your heart open and approach them with love, care and respect. It might sound simple, but it's all too easy to become snippy, mean and short-tempered in long-term relationships.
• Appreciate your partner for who they already are. You chose this person, and so they're a direct reflection of you. In and out of the bedroom, offer sincere praise and admiration. These words and gestures will go a long way.
• Give your partner the freedom to be themselves. Resist the urge to control and micro-manage, and instead allow them space to make decisions, own their leadership and rise to the occasion of your love.

On being fucked

In a lot of the conversations we've had over the years, there seems to be a common experience that comes up: women are afraid to be fully fucked, because being fully fucked has usually meant getting fucked over. A woman may share with us that she doesn't know how to lie back, relax and trust, because in the past this hasn't necessarily been safe or of service to her thriving. She's been taken from, shamed and made afraid, and so now, within the expanse of a loving relationship, the energy of this memory (whether hers, witnessed or inherited) lingers and drives the sexual ship in a direction that's not satisfying or elevated for her.

Another huge factor for women when it comes to thriving in the bedroom is dependent on whether they feel fully expressed, witnessed and safe in other dimensions of their relationship and life. If they feel closed off in general, opening up and getting fucked is probably going to be a challenge.

Because being the receiver – or the one being fucked – has been positioned as the subordinate role in the contrived hierarchy of the sexes, then within both beings during sex, there's this edge of misalignment where they don't fully know their roles or how to embody them with ease and empowerment.

In order to have elevated sex, women need to feel safe being fucked. A woman can, of course, also be the one doing the fucking – riding the other, giving it to them as the dominant – but for her essence to be fully witnessed and expressed, she needs to be penetrated. Deep in her pussy, deep in her heart, she needs to be able to receive pleasure and love. It's as simple and basic as that.

How to get fucked and feel powerful receiving

Let's face it, letting yourself take it can feel like the most vulnerable, scary thing. Whether you're the one fucking or the one being fucked, here are some tips to create a safe and pleasurable experience:

- Communicate intentions and needs in advance.
- Say what you're afraid of. For example: the fucked might be afraid of getting hurt, and the fucker of not knowing how to truly care for their partner.
- Find a position that feels good for both people and then stick with it for a while; take your time and let it unfold so that you can get to a place of release where there's more space to truly open up and go deep.
- If you need to pause and it feels okay to do so, pause and stay. Instead of pulling out or completely separating, stop the motion but stay connected. Speak about what's happening.
- Be detectives, and don't be afraid to try things, scrap them and then try something else. This is a process of learning and opening up. You can't get it wrong. Stay in your heart, go slow and listen to yourself and one another.

If one person is the fucker and the other is the fucked, then we need both people to know how to do this from a place of integrity and power. If women are meant to take it while men are meant to give it (in typical hetero dynamics), then we need both these actions and energies to be respected and understood instead of distorted and placed in some sort of hierarchy. Nobody's position is 'better' in the bedroom. Being fucked or being the fucker – neither person has more power, because they're both required to create the whole experience.

Fuck yourself whole

We need to screw ourselves back into our centres. We need to allow sex to resolve the imbalances and corruptions of our time. We can do this by having sex with the intention of unpacking these issues, healing them, allowing us to integrate and thrive. Sex doesn't have to be the place we come to after it's all figured out; it can be the place we come together to solve these issues.

What would it look like to come to sex – with yourself or with a partner – with the intention of restoring yourself to sexual sovereignty?

You might be wondering: 'But how can I restore myself to something I've never experienced?'

This blueprint might not be cognitively known to you, but it is primally understood. Deep down, you know how to be a fully expressed, wild, sexual woman, one who stands in integrity and authenticity. It might seem foreign or confronting, but that's because it's been shadowed and distorted, not because it's outside of you or unknown to you on a soul level.

You are a sexual being, made of sex, thriving through sexual expression. This has been corrupted by external systems that can't really be seen but are embodied and upheld by our beliefs and actions. In order to come into the fullness of yourself, you have to confront your embodied misogyny and the fear you have of your own sexual power.

Incantation for the sexually liberated woman

Take a deep breath and say these words quietly in your heart, or, better yet, out loud.

'My sexuality is a superpower. Although it has been shamed in the past, I no longer tolerate feeling small or scared when it comes to my pleasure, my desire, my body or sex. I forgive myself. I release judgements on who I am. I let my heart open to receive more. I let my legs open to receive more. I am ready now to claim this next chapter as a sexually elevated woman who knows what she wants and how to get it.'

You are a sexual being. You are a sexual powerhouse. This isn't for some women and not others. And this isn't just for the stereotypical image of what it looks like to be a sexual being. Remember: all of that is part of the illusion, too.

The truth is, you've probably never experienced the full scope of your sexual potential. You may have touched the tip, but like an iceberg, there's another ninety per cent below the surface, waiting to be fucked. It makes total sense, too, that part of you can't be bothered or has found sex confusing in the past. Maybe you're apathetic about the whole ordeal because, for far too long, you've unknowingly given away your power, and sex hasn't been about you, your pleasure, your desire or your thriving. Why in the hell would you want to participate in any of that?

But this is elevated sex, not the previous brand that kind of sucked. This is 100 per cent about you: it's about you finding yourself through the journey of sex instead of showing up when you're perfect and ready to go.

It's messy, too. It will push you outside your comfort zone and show you things you've perhaps never seen or experienced. But if you're willing, if your heart is open and you're ready to begin the journey to opening your pussy fully, then your life is already changing (right now, as you read this). Your mindset, the way you view yourself and the world, is reconfiguring.

You as a feminine essence being are moving now from the sidelines to a central position, both in your personal narrative and in the story that's written and makes up this world.

It's time to fuck yourself whole. To let all the fractured parts of you, or the bits that feel messy, unwelcome or broken, come out and dance. To heal and express through the juicy throes of your sexuality. What a fucking time to be a woman.

LACEY

I remember talking to a friend years ago about penetration. Is it pleasure or pain, we wondered? Was sex about us, or just for men? All messaging in my life had taught me sex was a service women gave to men, and we were lucky if we enjoyed it too. I thought that was the way it was. I studied feminism at university and remembered a queasy feeling when we looked at academic articles calling for women to leave behind baby-making in favour of more intellectual pursuits. At the time, I wasn't thinking of children, but it made me feel uncomfortable. I didn't have language for it, but there was a part of me that knew the direction we were headed, where women wanted to forgo their bodies, was a problem. At the time, I had horrendous periods, was on hormonal contraceptive and was living the standard, striving life of working hard, bypassing my needs, slamming coffee and getting drunk on the weekends, all with the singular focus on 'success' and 'making it'.

But what was successful about any of that? I didn't know myself, I thought my body was a problem, I believed the only way to have value was to work my ass off, and I knew having kids was both scary and an easy way to derail my life. But as the years went on, the misalignment became chasmic. I couldn't continue living out of integrity with my true feminine nature: the deeply intuitive, embodied aspects that I'd never cultivated but that wanted all my attention.

Eventually, I'd go on to heal my periods and leave behind menstrual pain. I'd leave behind hormonal birth control, become an advocate for empowered, autonomous birth, devote myself to sexual liberation (in its truest form), and then dedicate myself to helping other women do the same. I want you to know that I have walked the path, from disembodied to finally alive in myself, from pain-ridden to wonderful periods and sex, and ultimately being fully alive and joyous in my sexual expression. I still face challenges along the path. My journey is in no way complete. I continue to walk this path alongside you, and I imagine I will for the rest of my life.

———————————— 9 ————————————

The biggest issues for women in the bedroom, distilled

- Understanding the feminine and what's happened for women in terms of power structures and the hierarchy of the sexes is integral to understanding why many women aren't enjoying sex.
- Women have been performing their sexual expression, taking on their sexuality from the outside instead of it being born from within. It's time for women to embody and unleash their authentic sexual expression.
- Women are innately sexual beings (even when they don't feel like it). It's possible to wake up your pussy and ignite your sexual energy to feel more alive across every facet of life.
- True reciprocity is essential in order for women to feel safe, seen and open to letting go and becoming fully engaged and lit up by sex.
- Learning together how to fuck and be fucked allows for more love, pleasure and safety to arise in a relationship.

8

The biggest issues for men in the bedroom

Men, glorious men. All you brothers, fathers, sons and uncles out there, it's your time in the spotlight. Saddle up, because we're about to dive in and explore some key pillars of being a manly man. If you're a woman reading this, there's much to learn so you can better understand and relate to the men in your life. If you know a man that needs to read this, please share it far and wide. It's time for a masculine sexual revolution.

Our culture has conditioned men to be productivity machines, generally keeping their heads down, staying in the realm of the cognitive, focused on solving problems and the task at hand. While men are geared towards achieving goals and outward-facing success, when it comes to connecting inwards, attuning to their authentic sexuality and sharing this aspect of themselves, the story is very different.

They have grown up thinking that expressing themselves makes them less of a man, and after a lifetime of bottling up their feelings, many have great difficulty defining and expressing their emotions. This might be fine in the workplace, where you're attempting to fit into a stereotype of how men operate in the world, but it doesn't help when you're trying to relate to women, who are often seasoned in connecting inwards and expressing what they're feeling.

What we need now is men who can create aligned, outward-facing action and thrive in their right-brained qualities, all while also living and leading from the heart with integrity. A balance of spiritual attunement and action-driven leadership is required at this moment for men to rise up. Our men need to trust their intuitive faculties, cry when necessary and express themselves more fully. They need to become emotionally mature, develop healthy boundaries that support themselves, their communities and families, and become integrated in a new definition of healthy masculinity.

Our world has pushed men into a corner, and now it's time to deconstruct this corner and restore harmony to what it means to be a man. In the bedroom, men need to diversify, moving away from being thrusting machines or lettuce-hand lovers, incapable of navigating their partner's needs, and fully harnessing big-dick energy (no matter their penis size) so that they learn to become masterful and connected lovers. It's time for men to bring the full scope of their beautiful selves to lovemaking and their lives as a whole, so both they and their women can live with more balance and satisfaction.

Caveman to modern man

It's time for a Lacey and Flynn history lesson. If we zoom back in time, in many cultures around the world, people lived in traditional communities large and small. Boys would grow up alongside their fathers and grandfathers, and they would be taught what it was to be a man both consciously and subconsciously. They would learn skills that would define them and keep them alive. Boys could mimic what their fathers and other elders did, and create their own definition of manhood and masculinity.

In many cultures, there was a demarcating point where a boy became a man through an initiation. This point in a boy's life was revered by the greater community and was considered a milestone: possibly the biggest milestone up to that point. The boy knew that at a certain age, in order to become a man and carry the honour of what it meant to be a man, he would have to be initiated. This would often mean going on a quest or facing a specific challenge, perhaps even in a life-or-death situation. The young boy would need to call on all the skills he had gathered so far on his life journey. This quest or process of initiation is what forged the boy into a man and taught him critical lessons that he would be able to call on for the rest of his life.

If we then jump forward in time to our post-industrialised world, we see the landscape for boys and men looks very different. The invention of cars, factories and offices has been a big leap, but in terms of our male youth and their relationships with masculinity, it has been a setback. Boys these days often grow up with their fathers away from the home for very long hours each week, meaning their connections to their fathers and the source of masculinity and teachings have been radically diminished. It is now commonplace for boys to be raised mainly by their mothers and by each other at school. This has been the norm for multiple generations, and as a result we have young men out in the world who have not been closely shaped by their fathers and have not been initiated into manhood. While women and mothers are a hugely valuable source of love, wisdom, strength and care, they cannot replace the need for masculine leadership and guidance in a young man's upbringing.

In addition, the modern man has also lost his connection to the primal, hands-on hunter within. It is no longer necessary to regularly face death, build dwellings or access one's full stamina and physical resolve in order to survive. Life got comfortable, convenience reigned supreme, and many of the experiences that once forged a boy in the fires of manhood ceased to take place.

The challenges today's men face are of a very different kind to those faced by their pre-industrialisation ancestors. We've shifted from a wild world where we had to use our bodies and senses to survive into an artificial world where men are more checked out than ever before. The new frontier for men needs to be self-development and personal growth; they need to break the shackles and free themselves from the inside out, establishing their own definition of masculinity.

We know, we know. You're thinking, 'What does this have to do with elevated sex?'

But we're sure you can guess where we're going with this.

The role of men has changed dramatically since the dawn of humanity. Even if we just look at the last hundred years, and the way the family unit is now shaped, with men working longer hours than ever before and boys spending less time than ever with their fathers, we can begin piecing together the challenges modern men face when it comes to relating. If the majority of relationships rely on the masculine and feminine being in balance, but men aren't connected to their masculine because they lacked a father to lead the way and so lived devoid of embodied tasks that give the masculine a sense of purpose and mission, how do you think this translates to harmonious sexual expression?

Boys, men and leadership

As it stands in most Western cultures, there are no initiations to take our youth from boyhood to manhood. There's no demarcating line of facing death at the hands of a big hunt, no introduction to the virtues of manhood by a wise elder to show a boy the ropes of maturing. The modern man has evolved so far, and yet this dormant and unchecked wildness and need for guidance still exists.

Because of this, we see uninitiated men leading families, businesses and, ultimately, the world. This lack of initiation into manhood is devastating, as it creates a breed of masculinity that's neither embodied nor coherent, and instead is born of values that don't centre the wellbeing of men – or anyone else, for that matter.

Men who align with the masculine need to connect into and express their wildness. They need their bodies to be online in order to feel fully expressed. Sitting at a desk and thinking things through will only deliver a modicum of satisfaction to men. In order to be fully articulated as a man, a return to one's origins is paramount.

How to go ape

Going wild, feeling free and expressing your untamed manhood is a powerful thing. If you're up for the challenge, here are a few tips on going wild, either solo or with some brothers.

Get out in nature to create a sense of freedom Connect to the elements and feel the wildness around you. Build a shelter, make a fire, carry logs and spend time with your feet on the land. Challenge and expand your body by moving in new ways. Afterwards, spend time in stillness and identify how it makes you feel.

Guttural roars and grunts really help to move energy At first it might feel silly or performative, but there's something primal about letting yourself roar, release emotions and drop deeper into your body. Express your anger and frustration in a healthy way.

Bring your wildness into the bedroom If you're in a relationship with a consenting and enthusiastic babe, practise exploring dominance. If you haven't been used to it, it might feel foreign. You might also find it comes naturally but has been repressed at the hands of being in your SNAG energy (which we'll discuss later) for too long.

Unfortunately, there aren't nearly enough integrated male role models leading the way. We see politicians, CEOs, celebrities and people in other leadership roles who haven't done the required self-work to transcend their own storylines or discover their own authentic needs, resulting in misaligned leadership. These men often speak and act in ways that demonstrate they're not conscious, emotionally mature or heart-centred in the least.

Ultimately, what we're seeing the world over are boys in men's bodies. Leader boys. Boy-man celebs. You get the idea. Of course, there's nothing wrong with boys. All men must start out in this tender and novice role. The issue is that young boys are still defining themselves, still understanding their developing bodies and needs, while needing to be kept safe and held by loving parents. They are not supposed to be leading the world. And yet, many men in positions of power around the world are still acting like boys: emotionally undeveloped, uninitiated and going tit for tat as they get all worked up at the slightest conflict.

This creates the perfect environment for toxic masculinity to be born.

Toxic masculinity is immature masculinity. It is the misconstrued notion of what masculinity is. It's this murky, stereotypical behaviour that we associate with men, but it's not born of integration or a deep connection and understanding of self. It's like a performance of what a man is without a clear understanding. If you took all the ballsy traits of masculinity without the subtlety and depth, then thrust this repeatedly on to the world, this would sum up toxic masculinity.

Pondering toxic masculinity makes us cringe. Not only because we're bored of having this term thrown around, but mainly because it even had to be born to begin with. Toxic masculinity has taken hold because of the actions of undeveloped, uninitiated men in power who have made a series of poor decisions and acted in substandard ways over and over again.

But that's not to say that masculinity is inherently wrong, or that men are wrong for being men. In the same way that womanhood has been diminished, the idea of what it is to be a man has become a trope saturated with negativity, conjuring up images of domination instead of true leadership and an inner-born power that serves to uplift us all.

We're sure you'll agree, changes are needed. And we're sure you'll agree that it takes all kinds of men to make a balanced world. All men can be great; they just need to know what greatness looks like – and, moreover, what it feels like. The first steps are quality role models and a connection to one's innermost self.

Male role models are imperative to a well-rounded society. Boys need present fathers who know who they are. We need men in positions of leadership to embody the principles of what we're unpacking in this chapter to guide and shape future generations. We need men to uncover their own definition of mature masculinity. No, we don't want anyone to copy anyone else or try and be exactly like someone they admire. What we want is for men to look for aspects of inspiration around them and reflect on what that particular role model is doing well in order to inspire change within themselves. The ultimate goal should always be to uncover the best possible version of your true, authentic nature and having a blueprint and guide is always of benefit. Sometimes it takes seeing a quality in someone else to spark our own ability to align and uncover that same quality within ourselves. This is what we're after in the recovery of healthy masculinity.

To reclaim your healthy masculinity, begin by understanding all the ways in which you've ingested and abided by toxic masculine standards. You can apply sexual storyline practices to this by unpacking your relationship to masculinity with pen and paper. Explore the ways in which you've been afraid to express yourself as a man, what you've personally found uncomfortable or scary about masculinity, and what kind of man you would ultimately like to be. Do you have any shame around how you've acted in the past? What can you do to learn new facets of yourself and uncover a deeper definition of who you are?

Men, sex and porn

Pornography has long been a normalised part of male sexuality. It's not uncommon for us to speak with men who are using porn daily or at least multiple times per week.

to masturbate quickly and have an orgasm. This has created a new generation of sexually active men who have spent more time watching people on screen having sex than actually having sex themselves. They've been able to scroll and choose the scene that suits them, prioritising their own fantasies and desires, all while bypassing the second human, who is no longer an equal participant in the exchange. Ironically enough, though, this second human – the woman, for example – is usually the one being consumed. She's used to elicit pleasure without her own pleasure mattering at all.

The portrayal of male sexuality in most porn scenarios is one dimensional. We see men arriving, participating in surface-level chitchat, skipping through foreplay and then getting out their penises to fuck for as long as possible. In porn, men don't talk much, they don't build any trust with their female partner, and no real intimacy is created. The man doesn't allow space for the woman to express herself before they start having sex, and his pleasure comes first, always from the pelvis. In porn, we see a literal representation of all the things we've been rallying against in this book: disconnected people having disconnected sex where both partners' needs aren't expressed, understood or centred.

Flynn can remember his first foray into online porn as a young teen. The fascination and programming began immediately. Even though he remembers having a short, albeit decent, discussion with his mother about sex, the subject still seemed taboo and awkward, so not many subsequent conversations took place. There was some sex education at school, but it was mechanical and involved no discussion of emotions or pleasure. There was no one in his life with whom he felt he needed to have a proper, grown-up conversation about sex. It felt more natural to piece it all together by himself.

Porn, for Flynn and many men, became an outlet for exploration and quick satisfaction.

Like many other temptations in life, porn is very addictive. It creates a cycle of reliance and satisfaction where desires can be met instantaneously without the need to reflect on another person. It's a single-lane highway where the man ingesting the pornography needn't think about anyone but himself. Paired with the visual stimulation component, where the entire experience is created through watching others perform, a phenomenon happens whereby men see, touch, feel and climax all within a solo circuit. This interaction is far from what transpires between two people engaging in sex, and yet the lessons embodied and experienced during pornography consumption inform the way men fuck.

Men have become accustomed to brief sexual sessions that centre their pleasure. They see women on screen and think this is the way women truly are. In sexual exchanges, they anticipate female pleasure sounds that mimic those of the female porn actors, and they believe a woman's sexual expression, on the whole, is like those they've seen on screen again and again.

Even if they're not outwardly saying they expect this, their actions show it. They're not accustomed to the pace required for a woman's true unfolding in the bedroom, they don't know how to create trust and connection, they're unaccustomed to talking and dialoguing, and they're sure that their orgasm is the highlight, the big show-stopper, of the whole event. Men have been taught that they're the lead in the bedroom, which is not conducive to elevated sex or a thriving partnership with a woman.

In terms of endurance – or mandurance – when using porn, many men go quickly, aiming to hit it and quit it on their cocks so they can satisfy an itch, then carry on with their day. With that, they are practising quick orgasms reliant on repetitive stimulation, having little to do with full-body pleasure, or a subtle, gradual building of sexual energy and stamina. Ironically, male porn stars who seem to go on for ages help to encourage a culture of men who can't pace their orgasms, pulling the rug out from under their women before she's even started to warm up.

All this is to say that porn and consuming sex in this way in order to stimulate masturbation and facilitate a quick cum is wreaking havoc on men's authentic sexual expression and, concomitantly, on their partners' sexual satisfaction.

The reliance on visual stimulation is a big one that requires unpacking. When men strengthen their need for visual stimulation to experience turn-on, they find it hard to be turned on without someone else there to do it for them. This isn't a problem in and of itself, because, yes, partnered sex takes two, but it creates an expectation for the other person to be the source of said turn-on. Remember when we taught you about being your own greatest arousal? Swing back to pages 201–2 for a refresher. Doing this enables a deeper connection to one's own unique sexuality, and simultaneously creates a deeper ability to feel sensations in the body.

When our eyes are being desensitised by porn, seeing every possible scene unfold to titillate our minds, it can then be challenging to have sex in a regular way with a normal person. And it can become extra challenging to have sex with another person without requiring fantasies based on pornography to stimulate the session's unfolding.

This creates men who are in their heads during sex. They're either looking to their partner to fuel them, or they're drudging up visuals in their minds to fantasise about while having sex with a flesh-and-blood human. This is crazy, we know – and it's super common. If you're a man experiencing this, you're not alone. And if you're with a man who is watching copious amounts of porn or acting out his porn programming in the bedroom, you're not alone either.

There's no use laying blame. Nobody was prepared for the ramifications of having porn so easily accessible to so many people. Pair this with our chock-full lives, and the fact that men don't have an outlet for their warrior energy, leaving them feeling physically dissatisfied and desensitised, and it's no wonder pornography becomes a quick, mindless fix. It's easy and it scratches the itch. But it comes with perils – on the individual level, on the relational level, and for society as a whole.

If porn is steamrolling your life, or you have a relationship with porn that's impacting you and your relationship negatively, it might be a great time to seek additional support with a trained professional.

Leaving porn behind is an imperative part of the elevated sex journey. Until you've got yourself sorted, you can't keep going on watching other people screw while you have a quick wank. It's not that it's shameful. We 100 per cent do not want to elicit any shame or have you feel bad. Instead, we want you to feel a deeper sense of understanding around your own experience and sexuality – and we also want you to feel excited, because now you know what to do to level up. We encourage men and couples to give up porn entirely. Sure, you can come back to it down the line for some added spice, but you probably won't want to. Once you awaken your own turn-on and find sensations in your body that were previously numbed out, you'll probably have no reason to return to watching sex on the screen in order to elicit arousal.

'When I was thirty, I realised I had been consistently watching and masturbating to pornography since I was thirteen years old. I decided to stop watching pornography cold turkey. My sex drive and stamina improved, and my ability to be present and really connect with my partner during sex greatly improved too. It was difficult to stay disciplined, but the results were revelatory and very gratifying.'

Liam (34)

Like Liam above, you'll probably find quitting porn and embarking on a self-pleasure journey as we taught in chapter six will give you an entirely new experience of your sexuality, desire and enjoyment. It will require a strong resolve, which you can generate by connecting to your primal caveman self, who had life and death as his motivating force. You get to choose whether or not you evolve from the circuit of quick satisfaction while watching actors bone. What will you pick: the death of unimaginable realms of pleasure at the hands of mindless porn consumption, or the sex life of your dreams?

What we're working towards here is an elevated experience for all. Something that actually has at its core what men truly want from a sexual exchange, which is real connection. Real connection doesn't come from performance – watching others perform and then mirroring that – it comes from confidently expressing yourself to your partner, accessing your own true desires and then actioning them through your body while you attune to and connect entirely with the other person.

The brute and the SNAG

On the journey towards elevated sex, we tend to see two main male characters represented: the brute and the SNAG. The brute is the guy who isn't tuned in and often at the beginning of his elevated sex journey. Because of this, he's probably not very sensitive to his partner's needs and more discerning of his own, and his whole sexual style is a bit clumsy and heavy-handed. He's not necessarily doing this on purpose. In fact, he likely lacks confidence and overshadows this with jokes, bravado or projections. He's not a bad guy at all. He wants his partner to be satisfied, but he's not versed in the language he needs to speak to get there (and she probably isn't, either). He's a pelvic-thrust kind of man, not always factoring in the experience of the person whose hole he's currently penetrating. He loses sight of her experience in favour of cumming, and she resents him because he usually prioritises himself – not consciously, but because he's sure that's the way sex between men and women goes. He doesn't always love the feeling at the end of sex, but doesn't know how or what to change, so he continues to show up in the same way.

On the other hand, we have the SNAG – the sensitive New Age guy. He's further along with the journey of elevated sex, but he still has work to do. He's constantly checking in, walking on eggshells and totally incapable of dominating from the embodied and conscious masculine. When a man loses his feeling of freedom and leadership, he can feel adrift in the bedroom. He's got lettuce hands, is a really nice guy and drives his partner absolutely crazy because he has no backbone or sexual character. He's gone so far into the realm of trying to please that he's lost the sense of integrity in who he is and how he should act. He's scared of being the toxic male, or the brute, and since he's not awoken to his own masculine strength, when he does try to act manly, it's usually a bit of a farce, a performance, leaving him feeling awkward and ashamed, and further cementing his woman's feeling that she has to lead and be in charge because he can't be.

Yes, we know: this is very blunt and puts all men into two categories. Of course, there are many nuances, and some men won't fit either of these bills, but we're sure you can see some traits of yourself or your partner in these descriptions.

Time and time again, we talk to women who can't let go in the bedroom. There are many reasons for this, which we addressed in the previous chapter. Now we'll bring it into his domain. How you show up as a man will heavily impact your experience, and how safe she feels in letting go and fully expressing her sexuality.

If we swing back into the essences here, we can see the feminine as the flowing quality and the masculine as the container that holds, supports and contains her. When a man isn't holding his pole, magnetism doesn't occur. She feels less attracted to him (and the same is true for him when she's not in her essence) and less able to fully be her wild and free sexual self. She is always on the lookout for holes in his armour – not because she wants to take him down a peg, necessarily (although some women are doing it on purpose), but because she's continuously trying to discern whether it's safe to let go and trust him.

Without his strength, she can't surrender into her full feminine. And if he's occupying the feminine in the bedroom, being a soft and overly emotional lover, she won't be able to sit in that seat herself, because he's already taken up residence there. On the other hand, if he's in the masculine but it's 'toxic', or else unintegrated, callous or lacking sensitivity, she will negate herself in the same way he is, bypassing her own needs in favour of his own.

This is a tricky one, we know. How can you be sensitive without being overly sensitive, strong without being dominating, or tender without being a lettuce-hands lover? The answer to every one of these questions comes from within, and can be found through understanding the intention that births the action and energy.

If a man is a leader, wanting the best for himself and his partner, if he's tuned into his body and heart, and confident in his decisions and guidance, he will rise into being an elevated lover. If he can attune to emotions without being run by them, express himself without getting lost in the words, and listen to her desires and guidance without needing her to take the reins, he will earn her trust.

We know: this goes against everything you've been taught about consent and feminism and equality for all, but humour us, if you like. It might just show you something about yourself that you've been longing to unearth and connect with.

She wants to get fucked by you without getting fucked over by you. She wants you to claim her without feeling entitled to her. She wants you to dominate her without harming her or prizing your needs above her own. This is the ultimate expression of manhood – finally being able to fuck from within, thrusting from a place beyond storylines or the intoxicating constructs of our time and the assumption that men and women always want the same thing in the bedroom.

It's been really confusing to be a man. You don't want to perpetuate this poisonous culture where women have been subjugated and harmed by men, so you either get really soft, or you stay surface level and just try to get by as best you can. We don't want you to overly identify with the brute or the SNAG, but instead to feel a sense of relief at understanding yourself from this new vantage point. And women: these terms are definitely not meant to be used to insult or belittle your guy. They're meant to be helpful, not a hindrance to healing.

Ultimately, you're an epic lover with a masculine core that wants to be understood, expressed and integrated into your every action. It will take practice, and that's where whole-heart communication, the SIRCH pillars and holding space will be really helpful as you bring this work to life in the bedroom.

Exploring the brute and SNAG

Reflect on these questions and write down your answers.

- Do you identify (or do you think your partner identifies) as a brute or SNAG?
- What are the best qualities of this type of lover?
- What are the worst qualities?
- What can you do to improve or evolve in the direction you'd like to go?

Elevated sex for men

What does a woman want most? The answer is astonishingly simple: to trust you. If she can trust you, then she can be led virtually anywhere in the bedroom: further, even, than she can imagine. But that trust is not just on the physical plane.

She needs to trust you with her full being, with her soul, with her body, with her full feminine energy. She longs to feel truly seen by you, understood by you and safe around you. She needs to trust that you will listen when she speaks, that you won't be egotistical, and that during sex, you won't cum too quickly when she's still opening up to you. While this is inherently simple, it's not necessarily easy, and will require all the men out there to boldly press into areas of discomfort as they rise to this new challenge.

Establishing trust

Whether you're with a long-time lover or a newbie, you can establish trust in various ways.

- Tell her what your desires and intentions are for this lovemaking session and ask her to share her own.
- Ask questions so you understand her likes and dislikes.
- When she speaks, truly listen to her. Get out of your own mind and stop running analysis on every word. Just be present and try to deeply understand the importance of what she's saying.
- Pay as much attention to her body language and tone of voice as you do to the words she actually says.
- Check in periodically from a place of integrity and leadership, not from a place of fear that you're getting it wrong.
- Let her know – and remind yourself – that you're not here to serve your ego, and that you're open to feedback so the session is mutually enjoyable and elevated.

Women are masterful at feeling. They are creatures of emotion. They feel with great power, great nuance, so it is the quest of the man now to dive deep into his inner world and uncover his emotional authenticity. When this authenticity is uncovered, it is felt not only by the man himself, but by everyone around him, including his partner.

Women throughout history have been unsafe because they have often been abused and mistreated by men. As a result of this, the woman will often test your resolve, test your integrity, to know if you are right for them. This might look like challenging you on something small, which you might take as a rejection. Instead of walking away, she actually wants you to pull her closer. She is testing you because she needs to know how deep the trust will run. These tests might go on for the rest of your life in evolving forms, but if you are able to understand them for what they are, then you can be in flow with it and begin to pass those tests and build that trust. She will then let you into the deepest layers of her being, where full, rapturous love can take place.

To build that trust, you must show up as your most divine, powerful and authentic masculine self. You must be a masterful communicator. You must know your own body and be proud of it. You must lead from your heart while letting your ego slip away. You must, at times, dance with your inner masculine nature, which is always trying to find a solution to what she's asking of you. Your unique and beautiful combination of all of this will help you soar to new heights with your woman.

FLYNN

I have witnessed first-hand men who are highly intelligent, are ripped through working out and yoga, have done a lot of personal development work and yet are unable to feel or be in tune with their bodies, and are completely lacking confidence. Sex and relating to their partner then becomes the ultimate trigger, something that exposes all their weakest points at once, and they are shit scared of fucking up in the bedroom. The focus for men going forward must be on mastery of feeling within their bodies, mastery of emotions and mastery of communication to build a deep well of self-confidence in themselves and a deep well of trust in their partners.

Masculine polarity

We spoke about polarity on pages 53–5, but we'll mention it again here because it's so important. When men get beyond the honeymoon phase and into the depths of a relationship, they can lose their connection to their masculine essence. Whether they had it to begin with is another thing altogether. Nevertheless, the energy with which they magnetised their partner to them can begin to dwindle. How this looks in action is a man not prioritising himself, his mission, his body and his support and leadership of the relationship and family unit. This can be seen in things like skipping the gym and lazing around, no longer putting in effort in the fashion department, showing little to no intimacy or love to his partner, not having the integrity needed to hold a boundary, or moving into brute or SNAG territory.

He may also stop hanging out with his male friends and lose touch with the freedom and camaraderie that a group of men create together. You need to always remember who you are as a man, and push through resistance that keeps you falling out of the spaces and situations that help culti- vate this energy within you. At times, this may mean saying to your partner that you can't do something, because you have plans with friends or a session booked at the gym. There may even be some guilt around asserting this bound- ary, but trust us: her subconscious will feel safer if you stay true to your own needs from time to time. This says to your subconscious and to her that you are working to maintain your connection to your best self – and ultimately, this is what you both want.

Polarity needs to be front of mind if you want things to last. If you have the discipline to act on all of these (and more), then you will win her over and over again, enriching your life and the relationship, and elevating your sex to new heights.

It's fuck time

So you've been bold and tried out some Cock Gazing. You've carved out time for self-pleasure and you're feeling its effects. You've brushed up on your communication skills and you're thinking you're a pretty good listener now, too. You've left your metaphorical toolbox in the garage and made a vow to yourself that you won't try and fix anything that comes up as you learn to hear your partner without always weighing in. And you checked your ego at the door and promised not to take anything personally.

You have a new relationship with yourself: you're in integrity, you have a backbone and you know how to hold space. You're probably feeling pretty damn pleased – and rightfully so, as you've really expanded your potential at this point. Now is the moment to begin navigating sex with your partner in a whole new way.

Through all of the above challenges, you've earned yourself a new self-confidence, and it shows. It's exuding through your cells. It's palpable. And your partner is picking up on it. You can now survey the land ahead of you with the wisdom of a weathered seafarer, and choose the direction for your journey. The bedroom is your ship and your queen is there, waiting to get properly fucked through your whole being. This is pretty cool, isn't it? You earned this moment because of the work you've done. You get to look around this space and soak up the spoils of your radically turned-on partner.

It's go time.

You speak with conviction. You ask for what you want with a new conviction, and it is felt. Your tone is different and your loving commands are obeyed. You instruct her to lie down and open her legs. Your new power turns her on. You say you want to ravage her with pleasure. You want to try on your dark lover side, too: the one that has been kept chained up in the basement for way too long. It's time for that guy to be set free. You give her everything. You pleasure her and you allow her to guide you. You don't get egotistical about it, because you know it's all part of the journey – and you love this fucking journey. You both do.

Sparks are flying, and you're only just getting started.

Every touch is pure electricity, every breath is pure, heart-centred passion. You are online like you've never been before, and you know that if you give her everything, she will give everything in return. You give as well as you receive, and what you give her is the most powerful pleasure of her life, which results in an orgasm that you weren't even trying to give her, but arose naturally out of the waves of ecstasy. She cries because of the scale of the release and the beauty of it all. It means so much to her. You hold space for her weeping, knowing that it's not about you, it's about her and her experience. Then she wipes her tears and looks at you with nothing but pure admiration. There's a fire in her eyes that tells you she's going to ride you like you've never been ridden before.

It's total reciprocity, and you're here now, as the man you were born to be, supporting your woman like never before, having the best sex of your goddamn gorgeous life. She fucks you so hard and so perfectly that it makes you cry. It's just so beautiful and pleasurable – and because of the work you've done on yourself, you can feel it all. No longer chained to the laptop, jerking off to porn, you have a whole new level of stamina. You monitor your breath and now you can go for a long, long time. When you do cum, you feel it all. All the way from your heart, to your cock to your toes. This is a whole new meaning of orgasm. And the scale of the release is otherworldly. After this, you are closer to your woman than ever before. You have created something far greater than the sum of its parts. You brought yourself to a free new world where everything was possible, and you loved it all.

This is the kind of sex we want you to be having. This is the secret to deep, meaningful, elevated sex – and you're here now, having cracked the code.

'My wife has always been the breadwinner, and I was starting to feel dejected. I knew I needed to take action to reconnect with my masculinity. I booked a fancy date and stepped into leadership. When we made love, she let go and allowed me to take control, but in a way where we were both equally honoured. We connected in the deepest way, and it changed the way I feel about myself. It solidified how important our connection is, no matter who makes more money or holds the better job.'

Finn (29)

The biggest issues for men in the bedroom, distilled

- Restoring the masculine is not only imperative to a man's wellbeing; it's integral to the health and longevity of his romantic relationships.

- Polarity, no matter your gender or sex, will probably play an important role in keeping the energy alive and the harmony intact in your relationship, in and out of the bedroom.
- Boys need proper leadership so that they grow up understanding the nuances of healthy masculinity, sexuality and how to show up in their leadership without being domineering or lacking sensitivity.
- Pornography has become a destructive force for many men, impeding their own natural desires and blocking their ability to connect with themselves and their partners. Giving up porn fully (at least for a while) is helpful: this simplifies things and makes it easier to begin the journey of understanding one's own sexual expression and authentic desires.
- Finding a middle ground between the brute and SNAG archetypes is all about deepening one's own emotional connection, developing confidence, communicating from the heart and showing up in presence and power.

9

Pleasure over orgasm

This is a big moment to flip the script, knocking orgasms off their pedestal as the indicator of sexual success. Sure, climaxing is a wonderful part of any sexual journey, be it through masturbation or with a partner. But in our goal-orientated society, people focus too much on cumming and not enough on the journey and embodied experience of sexual connection.

That doesn't mean your orgasm doesn't matter – especially for women, who have become accustomed to letting their climaxes fall by the wayside. We still want you to understand your journey to orgasm and share it with your partner. In this approach, though, we're offering you a new vantage point, one where orgasm unfolds as a result of the journey instead of being the primary focus.

Have you ever had sex that didn't end in orgasm? For most, the answer is yes, and for women, this yes will be more resounding than for their male counterparts. Sex that doesn't end in orgasm isn't a problem, in and of itself. However, for most people, sex without orgasm is considered lacking somehow. A woman might feel inadequate for not being able to make her male partner cum but is often used to letting her own orgasm slide. A man might be disappointed if he doesn't cum but will probably be used to his partner not always getting a win.

When it comes to partnered sex and self-pleasure, without an orgasm, it's fair to say that most people feel like something is lacking, or like they missed out on the best part.

What would it be like, though, to toss out the impetus towards orgasm altogether, and focus entirely on the pleasure at hand – the here and now? It's a metaphor for life, really, isn't it? 'Happiness is a journey and not a destination' and all that. But there's something in this reframe that changes sex entirely, and we're here for this transformation.

You see, we've all become quite accustomed to living future-directed lives: focusing entirely on some moment down the track instead of living for the now.

We defer enjoyment until we achieve a goal; we are willing to bypass our needs and desires until we feel deserving based on an achievement down the line. And yet even when we get to the end, we're often still not fully satisfied.

This path to orgasm-less living can be a hard pill to swallow for some. Without the big O, what's the point of sex?

Listen, we're not telling you to quit the orgasm. We love a good cum, just like the next person does. What we do want, though, is for this to stop being a key indicator of successful sex. We want you to stop focusing on cumming and start focusing on the path of pleasure. Note, this shouldn't be at the expense of clear communication around what makes you cum. Instead, this is an entirely new approach to sex, one where both partners change their focus to presence, truly feeling and learning about their bodies and connection in a non-goal-orientated way. And – ta-da! – this will often result in a more orgasmic experience.

The path of pleasure

What feels good in your body? How can you open up, lean in, soften and receive more of that feeling? Can you become enraptured and devoted to feeling good and let that be enough?

In our work, both personally and professionally, we've discovered a number of things about orgasms:

1. More men are having them than women.

2. People focus on what makes them cum versus what feels exceptional.

3. When men don't cum, the sex session feels incomplete.

4. When women don't cum, it's considered normal.

5. Orgasms generally happen in contraction instead of expansion.

Let's start with the last point: orgasms generally happen in contraction instead of expansion.

Have you ever found yourself focusing every molecule in your body on orgasming, like you have to squeeze it out in order for it to happen? Or that when you get to a good feeling, you home in on it deliberately to 'make' yourself cum? We call this focus on orgasm a 'contractive cum', while a naturally arriving orgasm without focus is an 'expansive cum'.

When an orgasm has to be focused upon to be achieved, this usually falls into the realm of contraction. The entire being of the person homes in on the goal, and stimulation to the body is done in support of this. Often this comes with tension in the body, a laser-pointed mind and repetitive touch to direct momentum towards the orgasm.

If you were to envision the energy of this, it would be triangular, with the orgasm at the tip of the triangle and all the energy funnelling from the base towards this one point.

On the other hand, an expansive orgasm sees the triangle flipped on its head. There is no goal or impetus towards orgasm. Instead, the person or the couple are the point, and in an upward direction, the triangle opens up ad infinitum.

Pleasure is the path to full enjoyment, and the journey of sexual exploration is about awakening to all dimensions of pleasure. Tension doesn't arise in the body or mind in an effort to make something happen. Instead, the interaction is about not having to make anything happen; whatever wants to unfold then arises. This facet of elevated sex requires a free-flow of energy in the body and mind, which is leveraged through breath.

In any mindful (or body-ful practice), breath usually factors in as the main phenomenon connecting us to this moment. The breath – a process in the body that's always arising, abiding and ceasing – is thus one of the simplest and most effective focuses when we're wanting to drop from our heads into our bodies and promote a faster connection to the here and now.

The same goes for epic, elevated sex. Your breath is a magnifying glass into your experience, and an amplification device for your pleasure. Not only can you understand more clearly what you're feeling or desiring through breath-focus, you can actually augment sensation by breathing fully into the experience in order to intensify it.

If intensification is possible, then deceleration towards pleasure or softening the edges of energy-building is also possible. You can use the breath (along with your focus) to transmute orgasm, to create it, or to leave the focus altogether and instead be in the journey – and this is what we're after.

Ignite your sexual energy with breath

Before sex, use this practice to connect into your sexual energy and ignite arousal by focusing on your genitals. During sex, use this same practice to back off from orgasm, sending the breath and focus to your heart instead of your loins. If you want to augment your orgasmic energy, though, stick with the fanny and willy focus. Got it?

Breathe into pleasure

Take a deep breath and let it go with a sigh. On your next breath, inhale all the way down into your pussy or cock. Imagine that the breath is bringing energy into your sexual centre. On every exhale, let go a little more, sighing, softening your jaw and releasing. Breathe now with the intention to build a fire in your loins, establishing connection and presence to your sexual flame. Every time your mind gets chatty, exhale your thoughts and let them blow away. See now if your breath can ignite arousal and bring you into turn-on. Maybe you can get a little horny, or maybe even moist or hard, just by focusing on your sexual centre. Notice if you develop resistance or hit a point where you want to stop. Stick with it a bit longer. Let your breath lead the way into relaxation, presence and turn-on.

Contracting into orgasm vs expanding into orgasm

When orgasm is taken off the table, sex becomes about something else entirely: the journey. You might still find yourself cumming as a result of the pleasure, but it won't be that you tried to make it happen or wanted it to happen – it just did.

This is not something that most people are experiencing. Most of us are drilling into orgasm, holding our breath, clenching our jaws, curling our toes and tightening our abdomens to make orgasm a reality. It's kind of like squeezing out an orgasm – it's all very tight.

But what about opening up to orgasm? What about being in the pleasure so fully that orgasm spontaneously erupts – or doesn't come, but it doesn't matter because you're so enamoured with the pleasure of the moment that an end goal is just silly?

We're willing to wager that you've got a few tried-and-tested moves that you use to bring you to orgasm, and that you cycle through these – or some constellation of them – whenever it's time to get down.

Maybe it's a specific shaft-stroke that does it for you, or putting your full focus on the clit that brings you home, but do you know what brings you pleasure beyond the orgasm? What else activates your body in magnificent ways that aren't on the superhighway to climax?

If you don't know the answer to this, you're so not alone. And if you've never asked yourself this question, then we're glad to be here, helping you awaken to your pleasure potential.

You see, sex is not synonymous with orgasm. Sure, orgasm is an imperative part, especially because the biological reason for sex is to procreate, and in order to do so an orgasm is essential. This is definitely true for the male, and some believe super beneficial for the female if wanting to conceive, as orgasm might assist the body in becoming more receptive to sperm and their journey upward. Nevertheless, we think orgasm needs to lose its stature as the definer of what makes sex successful and worthwhile.

Sex is not worthless without an orgasm, just like life is not worthless without achieving any other goal. We need to move beyond the goal and into what's happening now.

So, when it comes to sex: what is happening now for you?

- What are you feeling?
- Where are you numb or disconnected?
- What sensations bring you ecstasy?

Successful sex kind of needs to take orgasm off the table to begin with so you can actually learn to be in pleasure in and of itself. You need to move away from the actions that result in orgasm in order to align with the actions that bring you pleasure.

'It was a relief to let go of the pressure of having to achieve orgasm and instead to be able to fully focus on the pleasure of each moment, every sensation and touch, instead of always having climax as the goal. My partner found it was much more relaxing for him to be able concentrate on just giving pleasure and not having the added stress of reaching orgasm.'

Latifah (45)

With expansive sex, you're opening to enjoyment. Your body is opening to what feels good and finding more ways to feel and come online. Through this expansive state, orgasm might naturally arise – and if and when it does, it will be born through opening, and not closing (remember the triangle analogy?). It will be born of softening instead of tightening, allowing instead of forcing, being here instead of wanting to make something happen.

Sex beyond the orgasm

When orgasm is no longer the focal point, sex can become about all sorts of other interesting, wonderful and fruitful things.

For example, self-pleasure can be used for healing trauma or moving through anxiety. It can be a practice of presence and processing instead of an activity meant for a quick release of energy. Self-pleasure sessions can be therapeutic, used for personal growth and self-development. They can also be used to awaken the body, re-establish feeling and the senses, and to relax and anchor the individual into their life.

Sex and sexual energy can also be used for things that may seem a bit 'out there', like manifesting what you want for your life.

We coined the term 'Manifesturbation'™, which is exactly as it sounds: using self-pleasure to manifest and co-create the life of your dreams. If sexual energy can be used to create the most substantial thing on earth – life – then why shouldn't it be used to create and align to other extraordinary creative pursuits, like aspirational visions, unfolding your dream life or earning specific sums of money?

We know, manifestation gets a bad rap to begin with. But manifestation is not about Ferraris and vision boards (although that might be part of your journey). Manifestation is actually about radical self-responsibility. It's a process of attunement and alignment, trusting yourself and the unfolding of your life, believing in your desires, embodying your highest self, and believing that you're worthy and that what you want is possible and inevitable.

In a world where we've been taught that everything worthwhile has to come through hard graft and suffering, manifestation can seem like a cheap trick to convince us otherwise. But for us, the proof is in the pudding.

We've envisioned and aligned to exact sums of money through sex, then had them arrive in our lives. In fact, the very book you're holding is the fruit of manifestation. We've created two births by envisioning them, then using sexual energy to make them manifest on the material plane. The list goes on. We've had students praise Manifesturbation™ for helping them generate $1,000 to $500,000, even when they didn't fully understand how the money would come in. The practice helped them believe, and then poof: it happened.

See pages 270–1 for how to give it a go, and if you want to learn more, you can visit laceyandflynn.com.

We're big advocates for channelling the power of sexual and creative energy in the direction you desire in life. We 100 per cent believe it's worth doing the healing work to get through the construct that this is ludicrous, too hippy-dippy or a fraud designed to target people desperate to get out of the rat race – because what have you got to lose? The rat race? Sounds like a pretty good thing to leave behind in favour of accessing your power to co-create the life of your dreams.

Problem-solving through sex

We've found that sex is the perfect place to solve problems – whether creative or practical. The decision can either be made in advance to use the sexual practice for finding an answer, or finding an answer can be a natural result of entering into the field of sexual expression and expansion.

When done with elevated sex principles at heart, self-pleasure or a sexual exchange with a partner can help to clarify the mind and create space for the natural upwelling of inner wisdom, which is what we all need most of the time when it comes to figuring out even the most challenging of life's problems.

Just like meditation, sexual practice can be the perfect ground for relaxation and a tuning in to this very moment. Beyond the stress of what *was*, what *is* can begin to emerge.

On many occasions, especially during his time as a designer, when he had to figure out many intricate issues relating to proportions, production, creation and installation of complex designs, Flynn has found that sex could be the space not only where he could figure out problems that otherwise eluded him, but where new ideas would arise into his mind from within.

Since sex (solo or together) is the expression of our creative energies, it's no wonder that other creative ideas and
pursuits can come to light while tapping in to this powerful space.

You might be familiar with the concept of the chakras, the
energetic centres that travel the length of the spine. This is
ancient stuff, dating back to BCE in India. If you've partici-
pated in yoga, Ayurveda or studied some Eastern religions,
you might be familiar with the concepts. Each chakra has
its own energies and physical body parts that it governs. At
the lower belly and connecting into the genitals is the sacral
chakra. This chakra governs sex and creativity, relating to
the sexual organs. It is responsible for pleasure, intimacy,
creative expression, feelings and emotions, sensations,
movement and change.

When this chakra is balanced, the individual often feels
more in the flow of life, able to gracefully navigate change,
pursue and experience pleasure, be intimate, feel creative,
and fully express their sexual energy. When not in balance,
or when not fully activated, these parts of life are impacted.

If we look at this with curiosity and openness, there's a lot to
unpack and potentially learn.

This is very much a chakra of embodiment, meaning being
connected to and living from the body. It's not about the
mind-space or thinking – instead, it's about feeling, experiencing and being. From this place, a new way of living
and interacting with the world emerges that challenges the
notion that the thinking self is superior to and reigns supreme
over the experiencing, sensually embodied self.

Ask yourself:

- What would it look like for you to trust more in your body's wisdom and allow this to come forward and lead your life?
- How would your life be different if you understood and believed that your sexual desire and expression served a larger purpose than simply getting off or procreating?

When you access this watery world of the sacral body and begin to attune to it, unlocking your ability to feel on an emotional level and also on a sensory level, you become a person who spends less time fretting over the minutiae of life and more time enjoying the ebb and flow while leaning in to the mystery.

We're not saying you should abandon your capacity to think and sort things out. What we are saying is that you've probably spent a lot of your time prizing that capacity, and maybe it's time to bring another faculty online so that you can live a more satisfying, enjoyable life.

Problem-solving through self-pleasure

Self-pleasure or self-exploration can be particularly powerful in slingshotting this journey. Partner aside, becoming the captain of your own ship, navigating your own personal blockages and becoming your own greatest source of turn-on is perhaps one of the most powerful and worthwhile things you can ever do in your life (yes, ever).

Because inside this realm not only exists your capacity for pleasure, but also your capacity to heal shame and fear around your sexual and creative expression, come to terms with your emotional and feeling self, and process calcified experiences that have long been locked in the body's nooks and crannies, offering a new level of self-trust, awareness, confidence and insight.

Who wouldn't want that?

The idea that connecting to your sexual self by touching yourself can bring more depth, love, healing and expansion into your life can sound a bit esoteric, perverted, perhaps, or simply too good to be true – but again, we've experienced it and taught it to thousands, so if it's possible for all of us, it might just be possible for everyone else, too.

Self-pleasure for healing

When you're afraid of something, find something uncomfortable or just downright have an extraordinary amount of shame and self-loathing around a certain part of your life, you've probably spent a lot of effort trying to avoid said thing.

Being in discomfort, especially psychic or emotional pain, is something we tend to try to get away from. Instead of greeting it head-on, unpacking it and working to understand and heal it, the majority of the time we find ways to avoid being in the sticky terrain of discomfort.

With self-pleasure for healing, though, we're training ourselves to show up for our pain gently and fiercely.

---- 6 ----

LACEY

When I was using self-pleasure to heal in advance of my first birth,
I discovered such a painful well of shame, hate and unprocessed
experiences, that I could scarcely believe I was the container for
all this shit. I had turned a blind eye to much of what was happening inside me on a pleasure level and a sexual level – and with
regard to simply being a woman in this world – that I was living
as if nothing was wrong and yet experiencing symptoms of no
sex drive, dissociation when it came to sex, painful periods and
checking out when it came to my sexual body, desires, wants
and needs.

Even though these symptoms are massive, I'd chalked them up
to the natural unfolding of a woman's life and minimised them by
focusing on other things. When I started to pay attention, though,
the issues were far from minimal. They were a behemoth, and I
was shocked. Amidst the shock, I was also relieved: relieved to
know this pain was real and not in my head, but actually located
in my body on all levels – emotionally, physically and spiritually.

It was hugely empowering to be the source of my own healing.
I used self-pleasure to bring my body back online, to heal past
trauma, to establish feeling, to process the past and align to
the future. It wasn't a pretty picture by any means (think crying,
snot, shame hangovers) but it was worth every ounce of discomfort. Because in experiencing and facing the discomfort, I was

delivered from being the woman who was ashamed of her body, had challenges with sex and felt disempowered, to being a pussy powerhouse living a fully articulated sexual life that centres me, my pleasure, my healing and my desire.

FLYNN

I use my self-pleasure practice to deepen the love I have for myself and my body. I touch myself and look in a mirror the size of the whole wall. There's nowhere to hide – nor do I need to hide. I want to feel (and see) the full splendour of myself in this life, and reside in a space of deep love and admiration for who I am and what I represent. I know – because I've watched my clients' faces cringe when I bring this up as their homework – that tapping into this space isn't something that comes easily to men. And yet, it's a space that has genuinely changed my life and the lives of those who have boldly gone there. Men's sexuality is a topic that doesn't come up too much, even amongst our sexually liberated friends. But I can vouch for the fact that cultivating a rich experience during self-pleasure can have a profound impact on your life. It might be challenging, but it's fun and free, so you might as well give it a try. Pay close attention to the feelings that arise in you. This is where your self-work begins.

———————————— **,** ————————————

In showing up and greeting her pain instead of running from it, Lacey was able to find new depths of healing that wouldn't have been possible by just talking it through. And this is the power of processing through the body. Sure, talk therapy, sharing and speaking the words out loud are all valuable and have their place. From there, though, in order to heal on a corporeal level and integrate the change into the cells, the body has to be involved.

Self-pleasure – the act of touching our own bodies and feeling our own hands on our bodies – is one of the simplest, albeit most illuminating, practices available when it comes to sexual healing and liberation. The second you place your hands on yourself, you understand why. Shame, the fear of being found out or caught, social and religious internalised messaging come rushing to the fore – it can be a bit of a minefield, really.

But if you think about it on a level beyond the story, isn't it fascinating that touching your own body, just laying hands on your physical form, can stir up so much? And if it can, then what's possible on the other side of this ongoing exploration?

We recommend giving it a go. Beyond orgasm, without the need to get anywhere, be anyone or achieve anything, touch yourself. You can set an intention for healing, or you can simply choose to be open and ready to receive whatever arises.

Self-pleasure for healing: 101

This is a journey of being present to all the shit, shame and challenges that arise on the journey of elevated sex. Instead of stopping when it gets hard, this is your chance to stay gently and fiercely present for yourself with the intention of moving energy by being with it instead of turning away from it. During your self-pleasure practice, think and feel into the following:

- What is coming up for you emotionally?
- Are there painful self-judgements or criticisms that you find yourself experiencing and wanting to turn away from?
- Can you let everything be present without stopping or shutting down?
- If you breathe deeply and ignite love in your heart, can you offer kindness to yourself and the feelings, ideas or memories that are holding you back?
- Is there something affirming you can say to yourself right now to set the tone for the new beliefs and feelings you want to have going forward?
- Can you slowly pleasure yourself and let this pleasure imprint you with a new energy that serves as a balm to whatever it is you're working through?

Successful sex for successful people

This exploration wouldn't be complete without offering you actionable tools to bring into your own sexual pursuits, whether solo or with a partner.

Fuck on a problem

If you're going to fuck yourself or someone else on a problem, challenge or issue in your life, choose what level of pursuit you're prepared for. If you're solo, are you ready to fully articulate this issue on the pages of a journal or out loud to yourself? And if you're with someone else, are you able to lay it all bare and get into the nitty-gritty of what you're experiencing and what you want to shift?

It's important not to approach this like an orgasm, with a goal of achievement in mind. Instead, you want to open yourself to the potential that deliverance is possible – and inevitable – if you move into your body, heal and let go. See the difference? One is the triangle that goes nowhere, and the other is the triangle that expands to infinity and beyond.

Once you've got clear on what you're ready to shift, invite in clarity. Ask to see the way, even if it's not exactly what you want it to be. Move beyond your own preferences into a space of truth where you're prepared – as an elevated sex practitioner and maturing human – to experience a deeper level of insight beyond the mind, the cognitive and the thinking self.

When you're in the throes of sexual expression, whether touching yourself or touching someone else, you don't need to keep bringing the problem forward. Instead, clear your mind, let your thoughts go and be in the experience of your feeling body. You might find other experiences arise on the body level, unprocessed bits relating to what it is you're wanting to shift. Let these arise and know that solving your issue might not happen in an instant; it might be a gradual unfolding. Hold the space, hold the tension and, like a curious explorer, do not shy away from whatever wants to be revealed on the path of healing and self-realisation.

Manifesturbation™

This is fun and one of our crown jewels. We've taught it to thousands, and just love the positive, powerful and playful stories that are born from this work. We'll give you some titbits, but if you want to go deeper with this work and be guided, visit us at laceyandflynn.com.

You can either decide on what you want to call in in advance of your session, or you can do it through the journey, aligning to it and allowing your desires to become clear. Some people choose a specific amount they want to call in money-wise, others are wanting to see the bigger picture for their lives, or change careers, or meet a partner – and the list goes on.

At its core, you're using the power of pleasure to create your dream life. Like we said before, it's not about sticking with the challenge-and-strife struggle paradigm to get what you want from this life. Instead, it's about unlocking your body's orgasmic potential and using this energy to open yourself up to receiving everything you desire.

Imagine that: opening yourself up to receiving everything you desire. Instead of focusing and trying to figure it all out, you get clear on what you want and start to envision it from a place of embodiment and sexual bliss. How much better does that sound?

This doesn't mean you don't also work for what you want. But instead of working towards your desires in tension, or in the belief that you'll somehow feel better once you get what you want, you choose to feel better now and wholeheartedly believe in your inevitable success.

While you're self-pleasuring or having sex with another person, keep bringing your desire forwards and let this desire turn you on. If you're with someone else, share it out loud: let it be hot; let it get you wet and hard. And if you're solo, envision this as reality. Feel it and let it activate your body. If you do come to orgasm, envision this desire moving through your whole body, anchoring into your every cell and then expanding outwards in a burst of orgasmic bliss, reaching into the furthest reaches of the universe, ready to be met, received and gifted back your way.

Fuck yourself free

We've said it before and we'll say it again: self-pleasure heals bodies and lives. We explore this various times throughout the book as it's such a fun and fundamental aspect of the elevated sex journey.

'Consistency has always been the most challenging area of my sex life. Sex would be in abundance at times, and completely drop off at others. Through self-pleasure practices, I've come to learn that the problem had always been the relationship with myself, not

my partner. When life gets tough, you get into
your head and out of your body, and this was
stopping me from showing up in my sex life.
By getting on a deeper level with myself and
regularly engaging with this powerful ritual,
it has allowed my level of self-love and self-
appreciation to increase dramatically.'

Carter (29)

When we take away the input of someone else and instead
touch our own bodies, we alleviate the exchange of energy
and instead get to receive entirely and give entirely to ourselves. We come face to face with all the stories around
self-pleasure and get to heal those, and at the same time,
we get to use the practice to heal the physical body.

LACEY

One of my international clients, a thirty-seven-year-old chief finan-
cial officer who'd fly in for our work together, had never been able
to have penetrative sex comfortably or easily because of tight-
ness and discomfort. Her long-term relationship ended because
of a lack of intimacy, and she came to me wanting to resolve this
challenge that was impacting her ability to connect with herself
and her previous partner. She'd lived her life believing there was
something physiologically wrong with her, so had sought out professionals (doctors, pelvic health specialists, an acupuncturist in
the field of pelvic health) to help her. She'd worked with a dilator

and done pelvic rehabilitation practices, but nothing helped. When she came to me, we began to work on her relationship to herself – to sex, to pleasure, to her own body. We uncovered shame, self-hatred and deep beliefs that she wasn't worthy of love or pleasure.

She began an exploratory self-touch practice, with no agenda except to be open, explore and learn. She did this weekly at least, sometimes daily, and really committed to showing up for herself. She also did Pussy Gazing, worked with me in person doing embodiment and self-pleasure practice alongside coaching, and came to a group retreat where she deepened her journey.

She began to understand her body – when it felt tense, what positions felt best for self-penetration and, ultimately, how to open up and receive. When the pressure around relating with another person was relieved and the journey was entirely her own, she was able to come to realisations and discover things she'd never discovered before. She was able to open up in ways she never had – to open her pussy to receive and to open her heart to love, love from herself and love from others. She became more confident in her body and learned that she wasn't broken and didn't have anything physically wrong with her. Instead, she needed to love herself and learn to connect with her body, desires and pleasure in newfound ways. She learned to be penetrated, to open up and be the woman she wanted to be.

The sexual body needs our attention, not just the attention of someone else. When we take our own healing, pleasure and desire into our own hands and hearts, not only do we discover things we might never have discovered, we also empower ourselves to be our own healers and practitioners. In a time where deferring has become the norm, self-responsibility is a powerful act indeed. Of course, there are times when sourcing outside help is imperative, and only you can make that call. But there are also plenty of times in life when your hands and your touch can be the catalyst for deep healing, personal growth and transformation, especially on the path of elevated sex.

Pleasure over orgasm, distilled

- Moving beyond a goal doesn't mean you don't come to terms with your own orgasm and how to have one. Instead, it's about moving beyond the goal into a journey-centric approach to sex and pleasure.
- Connecting to the breath in an intentional way can facilitate turn-on in advance of sex. It can also help with mandurance and backing off when the orgasm gets close, or it can be used to increase the energy and make an experience more orgasmic for women and men alike.
- Contracting into orgasm vs expanding offers two different approaches that can change not only the way we cum, but the way we live.
- Problem-solving and healing can happen during sex if we choose to use sex as the place to work through things and explore ourselves more deeply, instead of just using it as the place we come to when we're feeling hot and happy.

- Manifesturbation™ and fucking yourself free allow you to co-create your reality by accessing sexual energy as the avenue for manifestation and ultimate liberation.

10

Have sex (even when you don't feel like it)

When we first began scheduling sex, we felt both resigned and optimistic. We'd been having issues in our sex life for so many years that something dramatic needed to happen to prove that we were serious about changing things. There was something in it, though, that felt like failing – what kind of people can't spontaneously make love and need to resort to scheduling sex? It felt like it represented both the arrival of proper parenthood and some sort of sexual calcification brought to intimacy by marriage.

LACEY

After our first child, I recall feeling like I'd finally legitimately bought myself the rights to a sex-free window. I remember telling Flynn to leave me alone for at least three to six months. It didn't dawn on me that this request was problematic, because I hadn't yet awakened to my sexual power, so sex was still disembodied for me in many ways. Sex hadn't become a place of connection and union yet. It was still a place where I felt taken from, so when I was adjusting to motherhood it was the last thing I wanted to do. I felt entitled to this sex-free vacation. And therein lies an amazing clue – that sex wasn't giving me enough to make it worth it. Whereas Flynn felt enriched by sex, I felt sex was a process of extraction, taking from me what I didn't want to give.

We had no logical reasoning or blueprint to follow that indicated scheduling sex would work. But we had an inclination that showing up for sex regardless of the mood might be a path to healing this chasm between us. We'd both been yogis and meditators on and off for the previous six to seven years, and one lesson we'd learned on the mat was to show up, even when we didn't want to. We thought we could apply these same teachings to our sex life.

So, on Sunday mornings in the autumn of 2017, on the couch in our terraced house in Victoria Park, east London, we began making pancakes and having sex. We'd get our less-than-one-year-old daughter to sleep for her late-morning nap, then either make pancakes or eat the ones we'd pre- pared in anticipation of the brief naptime window. And we would enter into the dance of sex and discovery together.

---------------- ----------------

LACEY

The resistance in those early sessions was nearly insurmountable for me. I'd spend the days leading up to a session mulling over excuses that might help me get out of it. I felt such deep frustration: with sex, with Flynn, with myself. I wanted sex to be easy and carefree, but it wasn't, and I had a hard time accepting the fact that sex was a problem for me. Scheduling it, making it a non-negotiable, helped me to understand just how deep this issue ran.

---------------- 9 ----------------

Granted, our daughter wasn't even one at the time. Most people would say it makes sense a mother wouldn't want sex at this stage in her life. But for comparison's sake, when our second-born was just six weeks old (by which time we'd been doing the work on our relationship for three years), Lacey was totally ready to dive back into sex – and the sex was amazing.

In the beginning, though, our scheduled sex sessions often went the same way. Lacey resisted, got frustrated, usually wanted to get it over with, and Flynn held the tension, lis- tened, and did whatever he could to help her work through her challenges. Some might think, 'Sure, a guy will do what- ever it takes to get laid.' But this is going beyond the desire to simply get off. For Flynn, it was something much deeper.

FLYNN

We had such a great relationship. The only problem was the lack of sex, and all the pain it caused us both. Sure, that could have been swept under the rug, but I didn't want that. What I wanted was to live a full and rich life, and that definitely included having amazing sex with the woman I loved. I felt that if I supported Lacey, in a way in which she hadn't been supported before, she could discover what was holding her back. I was prepared to show up in this way because she's worth it, I'm worth it and our relationship is worth it.

There were many sessions that ended in tears for Lacey. There was a frustration, a rage even, that seemed to exist inside her body. When it came to sex, there was so much anger and resentment and sadness. But why? Why did this natural act that's supposed to be about pleasure and connection feel so fraught with tension? And why was nobody else talking about it?

Sometimes, the challenges looked like vaginal pain for Lacey, or certain touches triggering memories of the past; memories that had once seemed normal now felt problematic for her. It was like she had to sift through a lifetime of sex being disembodied. And in order to sift through it, she'd have to feel all the things she'd refused to feel or face over a lifetime of sex that felt more about the man than about herself.

LACEY

I was angry. Sometimes Flynn would touch me, and my body would remember being touched in disrespectful ways by other guys throughout my life. It wasn't what Flynn was doing; it wasn't about who he was or what he represented. It was that I couldn't disentangle the past from the present, and I couldn't imagine that Flynn was different and that this could be different. Even though my mind knew he was different, my body was afraid.

FLYNN

I think men are naturally used to feeling physically safe in the bedroom, but women aren't. Specifically with Lacey, I knew she had experienced feeling unsafe in the past. Showing her she was safe now was paramount. It wasn't that I set myself aside. It was more that this was the work that needed doing. This stage of the journey required her to feel safe, seen and held, and that was my duty as her husband – to help her feel these things so she could start to heal. I had to show up for her again and again, so that trust and safety could be established.

We wondered if sex could be the place where we healed the past and created a new way forwards – one where sex was equally about the two of us, and where we both felt our needs and desires were met. Even though it was awkward and uncomfortable, we persisted with our scheduled sex sessions. We showed up every week, no matter the mood, and treated the act of lovemaking like a practice, a devotion. And it worked.

Screw 'the mood'

One of the first things people usually ask is, 'What happens if you don't feel like it? What happens if you're not in the mood?' In a TV interview, the presenter asked this very question after we shared that sometimes Lacey would go off to breastfeed during a sex session, and then return shortly after and pick sex back up again. The presenter was shocked. How could you be back in the mood after breastfeeding?

What we learned early on in our explorations of scheduling sex is that 'the mood' (we use quotations because it's not real) doesn't exist. Sure, there are times when your body might be more inclined towards intimacy, but at its core, we reckon the mood is a construct. And as a construct, it becomes something over which we have way more control than we realise.

Think about it: if two consenting adults in a long-term relationship (with careers and kids to boot) wait until both people are in the mood to have sex, they'll rarely have sex at all. If we have to wait until that flippant, illusive mood strikes, then we're basically powerless, sitting ducks, until we feel the swirling of sexual energy between our thighs and hope our partner does, too, at exactly the same moment.

It just doesn't work. If this waiting becomes the norm, then a disconnect develops, and this disconnect turns into a chasm over time. If you're in a long-term relationship and you're relying on the mood, we're willing to wager your sex life is suffering as a result.

What we practise in our relationship, and what we teach our students and clients, is learning to show up for sex no matter the mood. We talked about the concept of being responsible for your own turn-on in chapter three (see pages 95–101). This is a foundational element of showing up for sex no matter the mood. In this new approach to sexuality, you're no longer living disconnected from your desire, nor are you passing your turn-on over to another person. It's your engine: it's your responsibility to tune it, lube it and keep it running.

When you move beyond the mood, you mature. You claim your sexuality, you take responsibility for your arousal, and you become masterful at showing up for sex no matter how you feel. *Please note: this isn't about bypassing your feelings or forcing yourself to do something you don't want to do.* Instead, it's about showing up because you've decided it's important to you, and you're dedicated to sex and intimacy as a practice in your life because of the benefits (such as healing, transformation, joy, connection, ecstasy, release – the list goes on).

This is the *pièce de resistance*, really, and to make this an everyday reality, it's all about working through the resistance. The idea of having sex even when you don't feel like it is triggering, we know. Someone fumed online about how un-progressive we are for forcing people to be 'willingly available for sex even if we're not'. We get this is a tough one at first. Many people, particularly women, feel forced every day to have sex – either aggressively or subtly – and so this reframe can feel uncomfortable. What one needs to understand, though, is that this isn't about forcing yourself to do anything you don't want to do. If you well and truly don't want to have sex, then don't. But if, deep down, you want to put in the work, then you just need the tools to navigate all the sketchy terrain laid around you as a result of our culture, your family storylines and what your parents taught you, your past, and all the norms that keep many of us from thriving in the bedroom.

Sex beyond 'the mood' is enlightening, enlivening and liberating, because any mood is the mood for sex. Annoyed with yourself or with your partner? Have sex. Exhausted and feeling blue? Have sex. Anxious and overwhelmed? Have sex. Desperate for a promotion at work? Have sex. What you need to get right now, though, is that we don't want you showing up to have the same kind of sex you used to have; this needs to come from a place of moving beyond the mood. We want you to create an intention to enter into an epic new sexual reality, using all the tools and insight from this book and from your own personal discoveries through doing the work in your life.

You see, when you allow *what is* to be there, you become free. We suffer whenever we want *what is* to be different. How many times have you believed that your current mood or embodied experience wasn't conducive to lovemaking? How many times have you felt annoyed or aggravated that you weren't quite wet enough, hard enough, turned on enough, and then battled with your body, believing yourself to be broken? How many times have you thought your libido is just different from everyone else's? When you stop fighting the truth of the moment and allow the truth of the moment to be the entry point instead of the barrier, you become free. Your life, messy or mundane, is fertile ground for creating an elevated sex life – instead of being the reason your sex life isn't quite working.

The crux

Most women are having performative, unsatisfying sex. Most men only know how to have physical sex that's goal-orientated towards an orgasm. After the honeymoon stage wears off, this kind of cum-centric sex isn't interesting for women (it might not be fully interesting to men, either, but at least it scratches an itch). These women then reject their men because their men don't know how to give them what they want. Neither party is privy to their own well of deeper feelings, how to access them or what to do about them; all they know is they're unhappy with one another and the situation.

The women have the compacted challenge of having engaged in a lifetime of performative sex, which gets registered in the body as disconnection and disembodiment, making it hard to connect authentically until these past experiences are recognised and processed. They also have the implication of sexual trauma to add to the equation, whether experienced or witnessed, which creates a subterranean fear of sex and a lingering feeling that they're not safe, even when on the surface they know they are. Women haven't known how to claim their desire or feel safe and comfortable asking for what they need and want.

Men have the challenge of typically being seen as the aggressor or as a toxic dominant, so even when they're not perpetuating this role, they're not always seen as safe, and their advances can be misconstrued because of said storyline. In addition, men aren't experienced in the realm of emotional and soul literacy, which makes it challenging for them to communicate beyond the physical act of pelvic thrusting through to orgasm.

This whole crux is where things halt and fall apart in most relationships.

This is the point where sexual desire dries up completely for the woman, and the man then feels emasculated because he is no longer desired. The woman becomes irked about being desired in a way that feels unfulfilling on a heart and soul level, and the man is at a loss, unsure of how to do the right thing for her or the relationship. Most people will carry on like this for the rest of their days. Sex becomes an obligation where both people feel uneasy but are unable to explain or share why without projection and reaction, which creates a cycle of arguments that they're unable to move away from.

Did we just explain your entire sexual life in two paragraphs? And if not, can you at least see yourself and your experience a little bit in the above? If so, you're not alone. This is a huge issue for most couples we speak with, and what's required to change it is exactly what we're sharing with you in these pages.

Scheduling sex is a tool to get to the heart of this. When you schedule sex, you're forced to face the music. Your resistance comes online, loud and clear; your anger and frustrations appear front and centre; your feelings of not being worthy, of being rejected, of sex not feeling like it's about you – all of it begins to crop up for you to witness. Most of these feelings can be transformed during intimacy and result in a powerful new sexual dynamic, one that is often based in truth. This is where you learn self-awareness instead of reaction and become a great explorer of your own inner world. Of course, it's a huge process. This isn't an overnight fix. (You might find yourself spinning at this point, because you finally have language to explain a cultural phenomenon that's hardly been understood or talked about in the mainstream – until now.)

It's easy to run at this stage in the journey. We've done it. Our students and clients have done it, too. Doing the work on yourself and your relationship requires a great deal of courage, compassion and dedication. It's not easy in the least and it will test your resolve. It's crucial, then, to ask yourself at this point: Do I truly want to change?

Sexual freedom is not for everyone. People say they want to be free, but freedom is a place without limits and we've all become so accustomed to limitations that when the walls and roof blow off, we can scurry in fear, trying to find another box to keep us contained and safe. The thing with sexual liberation is that it not only frees you in the bedroom, it frees you in all other parts of life, too.

We'll say it again and again: your sexual energy is your creative life-force. If that still sounds too out there, just think about your unique situation: if something isn't working in your life, is it best to keep going with it or try something new? Sexual expression is about pleasure, creation, joy, embodiment – it is the realm of the primal and carnal. The depths are untouched by most, and sometimes demonised or made perverse by those afraid of their own sexual nature (see page 90). What we want most, though, is for you to begin understanding how your sexual expression is linked to your expression across all other facets of this life. When you become free sexually, you become confident, alive, sensual, embodied, expressive – it is a key to you being your whole self in many ways. That's why this work is so important. And that's why you need to start showing up and scheduling sex.

Your sex, scheduled

The power of setting aside time to have sex each week means a) you know something is actually going to happen, and b) you know when it's going to happen. This might sound pedestrian or like a total snooze, but it's actually a helpful tool, even if you're not experiencing a desire divide or lacklustre sex. For those of you having issues in the bedroom, it means you're taking action and making a commitment to yourselves and one another. For those of you who are doing fine in the lovemaking department, now you've got a date in the calendar to take your sexual explorations to the next level.

If you're in the Rejection Loop (see pages 65–71), scheduling sex becomes a sexual treaty: the one getting rejected can now rest easy knowing sex is on the cards, and the person doing the rejecting can let their shoulders drop, as the anxiety of being pursued goes away. We know, this might sound dire. But we've experienced it ourselves and have helped countless couples navigate their own versions of this very challenge.

In our experience, the rejector is usually the woman and the rejected is usually the man. This isn't the case for everyone, but since our work is rooted in our experience, we are most effective when speaking to what we know best. In this situation, the woman can feel safe knowing she's insulated from unwanted advances that have become tricky for her to deal with, and the man can begin to rebuild his confidence and reconnect to his masculinity, which has probably been battered after many rounds of being rejected.

Look, we know this might sound rather uncool, un-feminist and not progressive. The idea of being in a clichéd, heteronormative scenario of the man wanting it and the woman not wanting it, being married, having kids, doing the whole obligatory sex thing, made us feel like we'd somehow got things terribly wrong. Lacey once studied gender and women's studies at university, and shaved her head in a bid to reclaim her body from the toxic throes of packaged beauty ideals and what it means to be a woman. And Flynn never thought he'd be in a situation where sex was an issue in his life, let alone be speaking about his own experiences so publicly. We get it.

We couldn't believe this was the situation in which we found ourselves. It felt normie and basic, which made the two of us cringe even more. But the truth is, this cliché – of sex drying up in long-term relationships, of women not wanting sex and men pursuing said women to no avail – exists for a reason. And we wanted to know what that reason was, to unearth it, heal it and rewrite it, because once we awoke to its existence, we didn't want to participate in it or perpetuate it for another moment.

Scheduling sex for couples

Start by setting aside time every week. One two-hour slot is a great place to start. The whole two hours doesn't need to be penetrative sex. Penetrative sex might not even happen. At the core, we want you to engage in intimacy first and foremost, then sexual connection and basically being together without watching TV or talking about bills. You might notice as the time approaches that resistance develops and you want to make an excuse to not show up (remember chapter two). You might even have a really great excuse (feeling super tired, needing to clean the house, a big work deadline). Ultimately, though, these excuses are just more barriers keeping you from intimacy and connection, with your partner and with yourself. Sure, you might have loads of other things worth doing, but this will always be the case in life. Unless you make your sex life a priority, you'll always find a reason to not bother. See the excuses, feel the resistance, and then show up even if you don't want to.

Use the tools we shared in chapter five to empower your communication and elevate your dialogue. This is where you want to begin overcoming communication breakdowns, maturing your ability to listen and speak, and creating new positive patterns that get your relationship and sex life from where it is to where you want it to be.

As you navigate the sex session, remember that you've moved on from the standard desire to get it on and cum, and now have the intention of connecting, healing and elevating your sex life. This might mean no climaxing right now. It might mean awkward touching, loads of talking, and a lot of stopping and starting in order for both people to be comfortable as you navigate this new terrain. Remember, what makes this successful is that you're both committed, showing up and moving forward with the explorations at hand. It's not about having an experience that can be wrapped up with a tidy bow.

We've experienced the gamut – from crying and tension to weird penetrative angles as we attempt to understand our bodies, and deep and meaningful conversations as we've endeavoured to understand one another's feelings, as well as ecstatic bliss beyond anything we'd previously experienced.

If you're not in a relationship, you can still schedule sex with yourself. Self-pleasure is an important part of the journey for men and women alike. If you're feeling resistance to this concept and practice, then scheduling it is a good idea to make sure you regularly show up. This is a time to be with yourself and learn about your own body, including the shame you have around touching yourself.

Scheduling self-pleasure for women

When it comes to self-pleasure, we want you to begin noticing all the limiting views you have about your body, your worth, your desire, your level of attractiveness and your ability to receive and create pleasure. We explore this in chapters seven and nine, too, and want to make sure you have as many entry points as possible into this work (and your pussy). You might notice some numbness when you begin relating to yourself in this way. This probably isn't a numbness born of a physical condition, but one born as a result of being disconnected from your body. As you begin to touch yourself and explore your body in new ways, do it without the goal of achieving orgasm. Touch your whole vulva, explore and map the landscape, and learn what feels good, what feels 'meh' and what feels wonderful. Notice what kind of touches bring about an emotional response, and let these emotions have space and time to be released. These sessions don't need to be pretty, and they most certainly do not need to be a performance, for you or for anyone else. They can be meandering and exploratory; a journey to be unfolded as it goes. At the end of each session, take time to journal and reflect on your findings.

Scheduling self-pleasure for men

We're going to ask you to explore your body in ways you might never have before. Instead of touching yourself to get off, we want you to touch yourself with the intention of getting to know your body in new ways. Resist the urge to use porn, visual stimulation or imaginative stimulation. Instead, let the touch and presence be enough to get you aroused.

FLYNN

When I quit porn, I began to rewrite my experience with pleasure. I began to feel my body in a new way, to feel pleasure in a new way. Porn was keeping me in my head and perpetuating the cycle of needing visual stimulation to get off. I knew I had to quit porn to deepen my sexual relationship with myself and with Lacey. When you move beyond porn, you have to face yourself: your needs, your desires, your body. It's a reckoning.

When you have these self-pleasure sessions, notice if you feel shame or discomfort around touching yourself. What ideas come up that are limiting? What mindsets make you want to rush or not be found out? There is much to be learned about your sexual storyline and how you show up as a sexual partner through the journey of touching your own body.

'We literally went for over a year where we didn't have sex at all because I felt so caged. I didn't feel like there was any intimacy in our relationship. This work has been helping us both grow individually, and also through the connection we have together. We both cried so much throughout this journey; it's been very emotional. This work has brought our relationship into a more equal and loving place, where we're really living life fully.'

Giulia (32) and Matt (41)

Sex as a practice

We don't often hear about sex as something you can practise. Like guitar lessons, doing yoga or going to the gym, sex can be something you show up to and get more adept at; something you devote yourself to and then do because you've chosen to make it a priority. This approach of treating sex as practice takes away the charge of sex needing to be a steamy, hot interaction between two horny adults who can't keep their hands to themselves. Instead, it becomes a sustainable gesture born of a shared desire to connect, no matter what circumstances are unfolding in life.

Sex as a practice elevates the act into something more soulful, heartfelt and connected as well. If words like 'soulful' make your eyes roll, we get it. We're not used to thinking about our spirit's implication when it comes to lovemaking. But isn't it nice to think about sex and intimacy as something beyond the physical? Sure, it's also entirely physical – it's about two bodies connecting sensually (meaning of the senses) to create feeling in the body. But the soul, the part of us that longs for deeper meaning and deeper connection, is also hungry to be a part of the equation.

You can opt to leave it out, to deny this part of the journey, or you can recognise that there might be more to it all, and invite curiosity: explore and find out for yourself. Scheduling sex, sex as practice, moving beyond the mood, and letting the truth of the moment arise, are such powerful mindsets and tools on the journey to healing and elevating your sexual experiences.

We know these ideas are unconventional, and that you might have resistance because it's new and it goes against the status quo. But if you're ready, and we think you might be, it's time you get out your diary and schedule in your first sex session, so you can deepen your experience of what it means to be a powerful sexual being living life on your own terms, healing deeply and being the turned-on human you were born to be.

Have sex (even when you don't feel like it), distilled

- Scheduling sex is an imperative part of getting out of your own way, moving past a dry spell, dodging the impacts of the Rejection Loop, and starting to heal the chasm and any issues that have unfolded in the relationship because of a lack of intimacy.
- When you get rid of the idea that you have to be in the mood, any mood becomes the right mood for sex.
- Understanding performative sexuality and the ways in which individuals haven't felt safe, seen or

understood in the sexual dynamic unfolds as the couple starts showing up for sex.

- In the same way you learn any new skill or dedicate yourself to a pursuit that's enriching and fulfilling, treating sex as a practice will unlock new doors and levels of connection in your life.

11

Relationships matter

**What would our world look like if there were more
sexually satisfied, powerful couples walking the
earth? What would communities and families
feel like if both partners were dedicated to their
own growth and development alongside the
expansion and wellbeing of their relationship?**

Behold, the dawning of the age of the sexually expressed
power couple.

This is a reimagining of what a lifelong partnership can look
and feel like, and a call to action for both partnered and
single readers to treat romantic relationships with a new
respect and dedication. We want everyone reading this to
recognise that they are equally responsible for the health
and wellbeing of the relationships they choose to be in, and
that all of life can light up as a result of focusing attention
and care on the relationship.

Truth be told, there aren't many people talking publicly about how great relationships are. Most public representations of relationships demonstrate strife, power imbalances and dissatisfaction. Divorce and breaking up seem to be more common than staying together, and if you have a solid, lifelong relationship, you're the unicorn rather than the norm.

Isn't that strange that relationships – the act of partnering, being together and sharing a life – have become so challenging in our culture? Why do you think that is?

To be in successful partnership, in a nurturing and expansive union, a few components are required: sovereignty; self-responsibility; a willingness to grow independently and as a couple; whole-heart communication; individual soul-satisfaction in terms of one's own contribution and fulfilment of a mission; a connection to something greater; a realisation that you will be challenged but ultimately grow as a result of the union; and liberated creative and sexual expression.

Very rarely do individuals embody all these characteristics or attributes to begin with. Many couples learn them together as they go, unearthing themselves and deepening the relationship in the process. You don't need to be a power couple (or a power single) to begin with. It's a way of life more than it is a destination, and so requires an ongoing commitment.

But so many of us believe relationships are just supposed to work. We think it's this one area of life where everything is meant to flow, and if it doesn't, it indicates that perhaps the relationship isn't meant to be. We find it easier to turn away from the relationship than to turn into it, and this creates the dissolution of many partnerships.

Sure, some relationships aren't meant to last the test of time. Some people are simply not well matched to begin with, and this is imperative to acknowledge. We don't want you staying in a relationship that's not truly aligned for you.

However, many relationships don't stand the test of time because the aforementioned components aren't being brought forward by one or both of the parties involved. Somehow, in our culture, the most common model is to quit instead of digging into what's happening. Don't you think it's time to change that?

6

FLYNN

When we got married, we wrote our own vows. One line that we both often reference even now is our commitment to radicalise one another. We first read the word in this context while visiting a bunker-turned-art gallery in Berlin. Radicalising one another meant aiming to liberate one another, to lift one another up and to be a key advocate and participant in the other's expansion and growth. This promise to one another and to ourselves has been a key factor to date in the deepening of our union. We want one another to thrive and to be our highest, most substantial and abundant selves. This means that we choose growth over comfort, and truth over what's easy.

It's important to note that these concepts aren't dogmatic or rooted in religion. So often, any discussion of family values or the importance of union and togetherness is rooted in religion or a specific ideology for a certain brand of person. However, these concepts are universal – they are soul-derived and not doctrine-derived. They are written of a language that we all come here with and speak fluently, which is the language of love.

Letting love lead

What would love do? What would love say? How would love act right now, in this very moment? This is something we all humour and like the idea of, but often it can feel harder to choose love and let love lead than it is to be guided by fear, apathy or the illusion of separateness.

Love for ourselves is the first love we must master. We must learn to allow love to flow freely through us, as us, directed within and born from within at the same time.

Current conversations around self-love don't quite get it. Love is spoken about as if it's a separate entity, feeling or something that you have to do – 'just love yourself' – but it's more nuanced and simultaneously much simpler than that. (Holding space for what our human minds perceive as contradictory is imperative in dialogues as important and foundational as this.)

Love is a way of being. It's not a fleeting feeling or an emotion (remember, emotions are simply energy in motion); instead it is the core of you, something that is tapped into and then expressed through your being-ness. We get it wrong when we believe it's something we feel intermittently or something that we can fall out of. You can't fall out of love. Love doesn't work that way.

Love is the truth of who we are. It's our most basic, primal, foundational self. We are love.

It can sound so clichéd – we are love, you are love, I am love – but love is so much more present than we recognise. It's not a *part* of who we are, it *is* who we are, and we're always trying, either consciously or subconsciously, with awareness or without, to be restored to a state of pure love.

Love is relaxation, presence, compassion and joy. Love is support, connection, ease, grace and flow. Love is aliveness, desire, satisfaction and peace. If love were an umbrella, each of these experiences would be held inside it. Love is the best of life and self. Love is the self perfectly aligned to the self without fracture. Love is you, love is me – we are love.

But let's be real: it's a dark age, people. Sure, there's loads of light and possibility, like stars pricking through the velvet fabric of the night sky, but at its core, we're working through a time of challenge where love as self has been forgotten.

Not only do most of us not remember this in our minds, but we also have a hard time feeling it in our bodies. The level of fracture between self and love is pretty immense, and because of this, we have a lot of people roaming this earth with substantial and untended emotional and spiritual wounds, often without any awareness that there's wounding present.

Instead of awareness and understanding, we have apathy, comparison, competition, dissociation, disconnection and friction, along with all of the painful experiences that we make manifest on the physical plain because of what's happening inside.

And these experiences, these issues that perpetuate such strife – well, a lot of them aren't even ours. We arrived with them, in our genes, passed down through the generations (remember the storyline explorations in chapter four?).

So, in the face of all this, how in the hell is anyone supposed to be on an even keel and create a thriving, elevated part-nership with another human? What chance do we stand?

Well, it's not impossible. It's just a bit of a challenge – and you're up for that, aren't you?

You come first

We wish we could give you a nice one-two-three protocol to give you the quick fix to epic coupledom, but unfortu-nately, it doesn't work that way. In fact, despite what many of us have been taught, most things aren't quick fixes. You can't 'hack' your way to this one, folks. Healing requires harmony, and harmony requires a balancing of energies. This can take time to discover. It's not something we arrive at, something we do once and then it's done; it's a way of being, thinking and living.

———————————————— 6 ————————————————

LACEY

When I dedicated myself to yoga, a pathway of connection, I was frustrated because I couldn't sustain that elusive feeling of awakening. I'd have moments of immense clarity, love and awareness, and then these would dissipate and become shrouded again. I was sure if I showed up for my practice and the teachings daily, that I'd arrive at enlightenment and be able to chill for the rest of time. What an adorable notion! I learned instead that the more devoted I was to my path, the more I'd awaken – and the more I'd realise how much more awakening there was to explore. It wasn't something that ever ended, because it was the journey of life. It was the path of love instead of a final destination.

———————————————— ————————————————

You sitting on the throne of power coupledom is contingent on you, first and foremost, being a devotee to yourself. From this place, you can align with a mate who's holding the torch, just as you are, and the two of you can spend your gorgeous lives weaving into union.

As you've discovered throughout these pages, elevated sex and a thriving partnership can only happen if you dedicate yourself to this way of life. You might be years into a partnership or still in the honeymoon phase; you might be freshly single or have been solo for a while. No matter where you are, this is for you. If you've been going along in one direction for a long time but want to change tack now, that's totally possible. It's your life and you get to decide.

If you are in a partnership, though, this change will require the commitment of both parties, and this is something a lot of couples find challenging. In our experience, we've seen quite a few partnerships where one person was keen to do the work and explore growth, while the other person wasn't. This is a common situation, and often arises when one of the partners doesn't feel ready or interested, not only in doing the work, but in exploring what's on the other side of the situation they're currently facing.

Because let's be real: even if something is terribly shit, you'd often rather stay in the shit you know than step into the void of new shit you don't. We are wired to avoid pain at all costs.

This is such a conundrum of our time: being afraid of change instead of delighted by it. But let's face it, change is tricky, because it requires us to do things differently, and we're creatures of comfort – even if the 'comfort' we're choosing isn't really comfortable at all.

So what are you meant to do if you're in a relationship where you're ready for growth and your partner's dragging their heels? What do you do if you're ready to be a power couple and your person is kind of 'meh' about the whole thing?

This is a big one, and at this juncture, it's time to explore your non-negotiables:

- Are you willing to stay in a relationship where growth and thriving aren't cornerstones?
- Are you willing to continue on as normal or is it imperative for you that things change dramatically?

Of course, these are answers only you have, and you have to decide the cost of both: the cost of staying and the cost of leaving.

And, just like everything on your journey towards elevated sex, you come first. You make the effort and show devotion to yourself, you lead by example, you do the work on yourself because it's important to you – this is what matters most. It all starts with you. You can't control anybody else's path, what they desire or what they're going to do with their precious life, but you can control your own (even the word 'control' doesn't quite encapsulate the energy that being self-possessed brings, but sure, you've got control here, to a degree).

If you're doing the work, if you're holding open the door with kindness for your partner to do the same, and you've expressed yourself, your desires and what you want for your life, that's all you can do. If your partner isn't interested in the path you're on, then you have to decide what happens next. Do you continue holding the door in the hope that one day they'll walk through? Do you decide that you'll stay and do the work on yourself, and love your person unconditionally, even if they're not devoted to the path of elevating your relationship? Or do you decide that you're done, that the relationship has lived its life and it's time now for the next chapter?

Only you can decide this. The truth is, we can't talk about elevating your relationship without talking about the very real possibility that your relationship might end.

On breaking up without breaking

'My husband and I are separating after eleven
years together (five years married).

'I recognise that I didn't feel fully safe in this
relationship to really open up sexually. It's like
the depth of the container wasn't there to hold
me. For a while, I kept trying, taking ownership
of my projections and noticing where I closed
off my heart. But it was like a whole body "no".
I feel relieved to finally be listening to my body
and honouring her wisdom.

'We are navigating it well so far. I am sure
messy patches will come up, but overall we're
committed to doing this with as much integrity
and respect as we can. We've taken each
other as far as we can go in our relationship.
It's a hard truth to come to terms with, but very
liberating at the same time. Love expands
and lets go; fear contracts and holds on. And
because we love each other, we're letting
each other go.'

Emma (37)

If your relationship is ready to end, it will probably be a
painful process, to some degree. No matter the current
texture of the relationship, even if things aren't going well

and you're better off on the other side of it, the process of de-coupling is still challenging, because it involves sep-aration where once there was togetherness, and this is a tender journey.

Even if your relationship isn't going to continue, you can still call on the pillars of elevated sex and all the practices, mindsets and ways of being learned through the journey of this book. You can be present; you can witness and listen; you can hold space and be an epic communicator; you can feel everything, stand strong in your integrity, and close out this chapter of your life with a level of soulfulness, aware-ness and love that will elevate you both.

Breaking up doesn't have to be about breaking. It can be less about falling to pieces as a result of strain or shock, and more about choosing to unweave the structure that's been co-created by the two of you. There can be beauty and grace in the dissolution of a partnership, but it relies on the partners to take this from a noble ideal and put it into practice through action.

Whatever the path, ultimately, we each want to choose to focus on truth and authenticity in our individual lives, asking ourselves, 'What is it that's truly right for me?' So often, we spend ages mulling things over in our minds, looking at all the angles and possibilities, when really we ought to be listening to that very clear, distinct inner voice that knows right away whether something is a yay or a nay.

We want to weigh everything in the rational realm and make sure it makes sense – but since when did love and relationships have anything to do with sense?

Love and partnerships are not about what makes sense and what's practical. They're about an alignment of values and about soul and heart satisfaction. Sure, elements of this come through the realm of the cognitive – we might love an intellectual chat, and this brainy element feeds our souls, but what we want to consider first before we go to our sensical natures is what the innermost self wants and says.

Most people know immediately whether a partnership is right for them. Their inner voice tells them straight away, in every avenue of life. But we've become accustomed to taking that inner knowing and filtering it through the rational mind. We hear the strong inner calling, and then we take it and mull it over, trying to decide if it makes sense, looking at the pros and cons, and, more to the point, wondering whether we can trust ourselves without knowing the 'why.'

The inner voice doesn't always provide a why. This part of ourselves doesn't need to know why, it doesn't need the next steps, because it's the part of the self that's able to live the journey step by step and trust the beautiful, natural unfolding of life. But the rational self, the mind self, is not interested in this level of non-planning, and prefers clear-cut steps: one, two, three.

The mind self wants to understand every aspect of the decision. It wants an equation that says, 'If I do this, then this will happen, and ta-da, this will be the end result, and I'll live happily ever after.' Basically, this part of ourselves would be relieved to know the whole trajectory of our lives, right up until departure.

But life doesn't work that way. We don't know what's going to happen, so we do everything in our power to try and know, popping our lives into spreadsheets, calendars and to-do lists in order to mitigate the risk of things going astray, keeping us on the tidy path we've imagined, where we get everything we want.

The issue is that there's so much we don't know. Think about it – or, more to the point, feel about it – do you know everything you might possibly want in this life? Or does the natural unfolding reveal to you more of what life has to offer than you could have possibly known through your limited experience?

Ultimately, love is the heart's language, and alignment the soul's. Connecting with a soul's mate or choosing to part from a mating that is no longer of service can be weighed with pros and cons, but deep down, you always know what's best.

The power couple

Relationships are the most important aspect of life. Without connections to other people, this life would lack meaning, depth, joy, growth and the mirroring of who we truly are. On a basic level, we need relationships to survive: we need our parents when we're little, and we need the skills of the tribe for protection, nourishment and community. Then, when we're older, we need a sexual relationship to fulfil the biological imperative of co-creation that most of us feel to some degree, even if we don't act on it. Following this, or perhaps weaved in at some non-linear part of the path, we desire – or require – soul partnership to thrive and grow and become the expansive and satisfied people we were destined to become.

Power coupledom is not about wearing flash clothes, making millions and owning a yacht (although if that's the trajectory of your power coupledom, then we salute you). This ideal is the skewed version we see through our commodity-driven eyes: the myth that says a power couple is one where two super-yang people shine bright in a public way and master the art of material wealth and money.

We're moving beyond that, to the depths, where power coupledom is actually about soul alignment, soul and sexual expression, heart expansion and the weaving together of two awesome sovereign beings who each want the best for themselves and the other person. It's not about what you have, it's about who you are and whether you're letting that shine brightly in order to illuminate your life and the life of the person you love.

In order to heal this world of the power imbalances, emotional immaturity, disembodiment of true masculinity and femininity, and the soul division that we currently see, we need to understand right now how important it is, from the start to the end of life, to witness, to be held by, and to participate in (to the best of our own unique abilities) powerful relationships.

Power coupledom is not about power over anything. It's about inner power. We need to move past the notion that to be powerful we must dominate, and step into the aligned vision that power comes from within, creating self-possessed and attuned beings needed by the world at large. This is what we're interested in. This is the business we're in – and we think it's a pretty damn good one.

Shared values and creating a strong foundation

Do you know what your values are? And, if you're in a relationship, do you know what your partner's values are?

Understanding your core values and whether these are shared will help you to better understand where you're both coming from, and how you can come more into alignment as a couple.

Sharing personal values

Sitting side by side, but with your own notebooks, take some time to journal on your personal values. To begin with, don't share them with one another. Write them down on your own and focus on what's important to you. You might like to pick five to seven values to start with, and write some bullet points on why you've chosen those specific values and what they mean to you.

When you're both ready, share these values with one another. Compare where you got to; look at where your similarities are and where your differences are. After hearing one another's, do you see shared values? Do you see values that don't quite align? Do you see values that are different, yet complementary? With your keen explorers' hearts and eyes, what can you learn about one another?

You don't need to share all the same values, but if some of your core values aren't shared, this might create an opportunity for discussion and a deeper understanding on where you both stand now and where you're heading in your relationship. This is also a great moment to step back from the busy-ness of life and get clear on what you want the pillars of your life to be going forward. Below is a list of values to get you started. Knowing your values is important; the next step is about embodying them so that your actions and life are a testament to what you hold most dear.

achievement	compassion	faith
adventure	community	fame
authenticity	connection	family
authority	contribution	friendship
autonomy	creativity	fun
balance	curiosity	growth
beauty	determination	happiness
boldness	fairness	harmony

honesty	optimism	stability
humour	peace	success
kindness	pleasure	status
leadership	respect	trustworthiness
learning	responsibility	wealth
love	security	wellness
loyalty	self-respect	wisdom
meaningful work	service	
openness	spirituality	

Relationships matter, distilled

- Becoming a power couple isn't about driving his-and-hers Ferraris; it's about prioritising the relationship and treating it with a new level of respect and devotion.
- When we let love lead the way, we become happier, more content and better able to see our partners clearly, supporting them on their own journeys as both people grow together.
- A successful relationship is comprised of two autonomous and whole beings. Remember that you

come first, and your power coupledom is reliant on you being a devotee to yourself first and foremost.

• Breaking up is never easy, but if that's the trajectory for you, it's possible to nurture yourself through the process and hold the other person in high esteem, even as the relationship dynamic shifts.

12

The way forward – the sexually integrated being

We have no species without sex, and yet we've somehow got it so wrong when it comes to the way we relate to and engage in sex, pleasure and intimacy. We've categorically lost our way, raising generations who feel shame, fear and a total lack of confidence when it comes to anything beyond standard bonking. But the heart wants what the heart wants – and you've gone on this journey with us because you're longing for depth across all facets of life, especially love-making and sexual expression.

The way forward is about fostering a sexually integrated society, one where sex stops being compartmentalised to the bedroom and instead is an energy to which we're all attuned. We know, it's an idealistic visionary landscape, but just imagine a world where sex stops being a power trip, a place of performance and uncertainty, an act only done under the ideal circumstances, and instead is a place of devotion, exploration, healing, play and discovery.

This is what we're after. This is what this book is all about: helping people realise just how powerful sex can be if they let themselves rise in power and meet one another with hearts wide open, ready to screw, feel pleasure, find ecstasy, be confidently vulnerable and be open to what- ever else arises when sex leads the way.

'We are more open with our communication about sex, expectations, likes and dislikes, and past relationships. I think we feel more comfortable as individuals and also together. Instead of seeing it as shameful or a duty, we now see sex as a beautiful way of connecting with one another. Because of this work, we hold sex and intimacy as a more sacred place than before.'

Aaron (34) and Eve (34)

The decompartmentalisation of sexual energy

It's a strange thing, the way sex has become 'other' in our society. It doesn't feel integrated into daily life and the public psyche in a healthy way, and instead has an air of shadow, secrecy and toxicity about it. Very few people have balanced and mature relationships to sex and, ultimately, to their own pleasure, desire and sexual expression. Think about it: even though most adults aspire to be sexually active, the idea of someone hearing or walking in on you while you're self-pleasuring or having sex makes you feel queasy. We're afraid of being seen in our desire and in the primal expression of our body's needs and wants.

Sex has been reduced to the singular act that is often expressed as something that happens between two people behind closed doors. Sure, sex, in its essence, is most often defined as sexual activity – and, more specifically, intercourse. What we're talking about here, then, is sex, yes, and also the broader expression of sex and all the structures that inform how sex is perceived, experienced and interpreted by a person.

On an individual level, this looks like a person who has read these pages, experienced the natural healing and unfolding in their life after bringing this knowledge into their body, and then finally has activated this work through deliberate and conscious processing and actioning. In order to decompartmentalise sex and sexual expression, we have to decompartmentalise our own sexuality, moving it from the basement or edges of ourselves into the integrated whole.

On the daily, this looks and feels like embodiment, meaning we inhabit and experience our bodies instead of bypassing them or seeing them as secondary to the mind self. A sexually expressed and thriving person is someone who is anchored to their physical form, no longer fighting their body or experiencing it as dirty, base or inconvenient.

We see awake bodies: women who are cyclically aware and connected, fluid and sensual, and men who are physical and dynamic, connected to their hearts and their loins. We move beyond a bobblehead world where intellect reigns supreme and sitting at your desk using your thinking powers for ten hours a day is a virtue, and into a world where we remember who we are: animals who require nature and physicality, lust and desire, creativity and play, to express the fullness of our beings.

As you become sexually liberated (and the world follows suit), you will feel free to be yourself in your body. As a woman, you'll be connected to your authentic desires, feel safe to express these and no longer 'perform' your sexuality in order to entice men. And as a man, your presence will not be threatening (even if you are a massive dude), because you'll be connected to your heart and you'll move from appraising women into a space of meeting and connecting with them instead.

We want you to imagine and feel yourself as this fully sexually expressed being:

- How do you stand?
- How do you hold your chest and heart?
- How do your feet feel on the earth?
- How does your pelvis sit?
- How does your pussy or cock feel?

Our lives must become more harmonious, moving beyond the rigours of overworking and under-creating. We must feel our life-force come back online – for the first time or again and again – in order to embody this sexual revolution.

In the past, sexual liberation was about having sex outside marriage, the institution and the need for it to result in children. Traditional roles and views were challenged in order for people to feel free to have sex outside dogma. This new sexual revolution we're sharing here, some sixty years on from the 1960s version, is a natural extension and deepening, and also a returning in some way to traditional values, expressed soulfully instead of righteously.

Instead of fighting for the right to have sex whenever and wherever we see fit and with whomever we choose, we're promoting a waking up to a deeper truth about sex that isn't simply about thrusting it out with anyone, anytime, anywhere. There's no judgement here, but usually in the scenario above, you're leaking sexual energy and not necessarily experiencing satisfaction beyond the immediate scratch of a horny itch. We've both been there. We get it.

This is about a return to sacred sexuality and soulful sexual expression. It's about animalistic desire brought forward through our amazing bodies, and satisfaction on the body and spirit level achieved by expressing our sexual core energy. Perhaps it's slightly more niche than the earlier iteration of sexual liberation. It won't be for everyone, but most revolutions aren't.

It's not based on dogma or ancient texts. It's not religious. But it is spiritual. Spirituality is the feeling and belief that there's something greater than that which meets the senses. There's no credo or organisation to appease. Instead, it's personal. And this whole journey of elevated sex is very personal.

What we imagine is that this book, on the whole, is some-how touching a part of you that already knows much of this stuff already. You might not know it on a cognitive level, but you know it on a wisdom level – the part of you that knows things just because you do. Perhaps you haven't given much credence to this facet of self, because – sur-prise! – it's been diminished and replaced by a need to prove and qualify everything through some sort of study or scientific equation.

But you know what you know, don't you? Even if you try to convince yourself otherwise, that deep voice within will continue to whisper. You might turn away from it again and again; you might mute it or turn it down; you might have even lost the volume control and find it hard to turn it back up after years of disregarding it. But no matter what, it's there.

What is the cost of going another day living as if your sexual expression is not a part of the whole of who you are? What is the cost of compartmentalising sex for another moment of this precious life?

Being sexual

For you, on an individual level, the integration of your sexual energy is going to make you a more powerful, aligned and authentic person: a human who embodies and lives connected to their sexuality has a depth that those who don't simply can't yet possess. When a person is living in sexual integration, you can see it in their eyes, feel it in their movements, and simply sense a more robust and expansive character in your midst.

It's important not to confuse this with someone who is simply overtly sexual. There's nothing wrong with being sexual and showing this, but there's a difference between mugging and embodying, between performing and authentically expressing. The label of 'sexual' – *she's very sexual/he's very sexual* – isn't necessarily the same thing as what we're talking about. And this is where it gets nuanced.

LACEY

I was always quite sexual. I remember sexy dancing as a kid and being up for all the sex I could get as a young woman. This sexual expression, though, wasn't mature or entirely authentic. I didn't know how to be my true sexual self, so I performed my sexuality without realising it. I was sexual but not embodied. I expressed the shadow side of sexual liberation without ever knowing I was doing it. I simply thought I was free and fun, which I was. But what I didn't know was that there was more to it than that. I'd never heard anyone talk about sex in a way that was holistic or had meaning, and I'd never witnessed soulful, connected partnering. My sexual expression at this stage of my life was a result of trying to bring forward what I felt deep within. Because I only had toxic blueprints by which to mould myself (TV, movies, magazines), I didn't know how to be powerfully sexual in a way where my energy was about me first, instead of being about me trying to lure others in or be liked by men.

You might not have realised you were performing in the bedroom – and in your life – until this minute. There's no shame in this recognition. *Smile for the camera, don't be sad, be nice, be a man, be a good girl* – we've been told over and over again in our lives to show up in ways that aren't the expression of how we truly feel, and so it only follows that we're acting out what we think is expected of us, ultimately because we want to be loved and accepted.

We perform in overt ways, moaning and asking for it in the bedroom when it doesn't actually feel good. We perform when we don't really want it, and we perform in the world, covering over our emotional and feeling selves in order to keep going, to succeed, to never give up.

We've learned to live so much of our lives for an idea of who we think we ought to be, to the extent that many of us have no idea who we truly are. We are, in many ways, separate from ourselves instead of in union with ourselves.

This cycle has to end.

This circuit that has us all believing that sex is an act you do with another person when nobody is looking, making sure never to let anyone hear you or see you in your most vulnerable, powerful and expressive act. This circuit that has us disembodied and dysregulated, unsure of how to be sexual without it being a performance, because nobody ever taught us or modelled authentic sexuality. This circuit where we shame ourselves, our children and others for their sensuality or enjoyment of their bodies, because this is what has been modelled and experienced by us all. It has to stop now.

There's no blame here. It would be easy to point the finger at your parents or society, at religion or institutionalised education, but really everyone is simply living out the unwritten rule book that's been around for ages. Yes, there are some people who are maliciously and deliberately upholding ideologies that repress, subjugate and disempower people from their sexual expression. Of course, these are people whose actions are rooted in hatred – but that's another story. We're talking more broadly here about the majority instead of the demonic minority. We choose to believe that most people have no idea what they're upholding through their actions; that most of us are scared and doing our best, and that even those who are doing a shitty job probably aren't doing it on purpose. We love the benefit of the doubt, and believe that most people are unaware that there's a saturated, technicolour world of sexual expressiveness available to those willing and able to wake up to it.

For couples, this looks like a relationship where sexual expression is alive and well throughout daily interactions. It's about all the pillars of elevated sex being integrated into the fabric of the relationship (swing back to chapter three for a refresher). It's about a connection to the emotional self, an attunement to the soul self and a re-sensitisation of the sexual self, so that we're feeling, we're alive and we're connected.

In a very practical way, this looks like people who are not governed by their emotions or stories. When something sparks an emotional reaction, the person feels their feelings without overly identifying with them. So, for example, you get frustrated with your partner, and instead of getting swept up into the agitation, you feel it, recognise what's happening and own it. You claim your frustration without the need to belittle the other person or bemoan the experience. You express what's got you frustrated, enquire into your part of it and make a request for what you need changed. You understand yourself, your feelings and your needs, and you're able to communicate them. Hello, whole-heart communication.

When it comes to sex, you can do the same thing. If you have desires that aren't being met, or you are processing experiences and need space held, you can own this and express it. You can become tuned in to your inner world and in charge of yourself instead of continuously being swept up in the fleeting expressions of an ever-fluctuating internal landscape. Instead of identifying with your sadness or awkwardness or whatever, you can learn to feel and express it in a way that's healthy and productive.

Now listen, don't get us wrong. You can still be a wild beast. You can yelp and scream if you need to. You can cry and snot all over yourself and your person. This isn't glossy-magazine spirituality that we're touting. We have no interest in your tidiness. We want it all: everything that's real, expressed in relation to the highest part of you. This is about fully embodied and spiritual consciousness, and living a whole – and holy – sexually expressed life.

FLYNN

Full emotional expression wasn't easy for me. It didn't come naturally. I spent much of my younger years feeling frustrated and down; an inner feeling of stickiness and sadness was often present. I didn't feel capable of expressing myself and I identified with these feelings: 'I *am* depressed' instead of 'I *feel* depressed' – that kind of thing. It took years as an adult to connect my feelings to words, and then to feel confident in articulating these. This was a huge challenge for me, but it's one I wanted to undertake to become a more connected man, and ultimately a better husband and father. I want to be the man who can talk about his feelings with confidence and ease. I want my children to experience a father who is vulnerable in exposing all aspects of himself. I want to try and model being a well-rounded soul. This is imperative in elevated sex: that men learn to feel, identify, apply words to and then express their emotions. It's been one of the richest journeys of my life.

In order to do this work in depth, both people in a partnership have to be on board. It's possible to walk the path solo, but for it to take hold entirely in the relationship, there has to be shared vision and commitment. Sometimes, one partner needs it less and another needs it more. Sometimes, one partner is a diehard sceptic and not interested in self-development, while the other person is open and ready. Sometimes, both people are in it and ready to jump. The most common configuration we've seen is an openness on the part of one partner and resistance on the part of the other.

If you're the partner that's open, keep going. Do this work for yourself, for your children (if you have them) and for your relationship, as it will undoubtedly impact it in a positive way. If you're the resistant partner and your relationship is on the line, ask yourself what you're willing to lose if you don't do this work in your own life. It could be your partner; it could be a lifetime of sexual fun and expressiveness. It could be shame or deep beliefs you've taken as gospel. Whatever it is, now is the time to ask yourself these questions, because your relationship and happiness might be dependent on it.

We can't teach you everything in the pages of this book. We've endeavoured to draw attention to as many corners of this process as possible, asking powerful questions and giving you some practices to activate in your life. To take this work deeper and make meaningful, long-lasting change, the best next step is to visit us at laceyandflynn.com so we can guide you further on the path.

The sexually integrated being

Imagine a life where you no longer feel shame about your body, where every part of your body is loved and accepted and seen as part of the perfect whole.

Imagine a life where you know what you like, know what you want and feel confident enough to go out and get it.

Imagine never feeling unworthy because you understand your intrinsic worth, just by being you.

Imagine feeling empowered to touch yourself, to enjoy pleasure, to heal the past, to claim the present and be fully open to the future.

Imagine being able to safely and happily relate sexually to other people, relaxed in your skin, not awkward about being touched or adored, and joyously both giving and receiving.

Imagine being sexually free – free with your core creative and pleasure energy, so that you can open up in every single part of life.

This is what's possible through true sexual awakening and integration.

You might have noticed the above points weren't just about sex and your relationship. That's because – as we've hammered home – this work gifts you full expansion across every part of your glorious life. Sure, you'll have epic, cum-worthy sex that's orgasmic and blissful and fun and deep, but you'll also experience this depth and freedom across your entire life.

Sexual repression creates dis-ease, and not just in the bedroom. We've said it before and we'll say it again: in order to be fully alive, you need to be free with the energy you were born from. Deep, meaningful, elevated sex creates a deep, meaningful, elevated life. It's that simple.

So, now that you know all this stuff, how do you become a sexually integrated being?

On a practical level, if you begin to ask yourself the powerful questions we posed to you in each chapter, answering truthfully, fully and without holding back, just that alone will blow your mind and begin to reconfigure your life.

The coaching methodology relies on you, the person being coached (if we could suggest for a moment that this text is a bit coachy), taking responsibility to find the answers within. Unlike mentoring, where you're given the answers from someone down the line (we suppose we're mentoring you, too), or therapy, which digs into the past (okay, we're kind of doing that too, but we're not therapists), we want you to feel empowered to unpack and understand your own life.

By starting with powerful questions, you'll discern where your main areas of tension or challenge are, and you can begin to hone in on those. From there, you can activate some of the practices we've taught in these pages to bring the material to life through your body. Granted, this book was never designed to be a how-to. It's a guide, a manifesto and a space for you to finally understand the secrets to elevated sex – which we definitely don't want to keep secret any longer.

To be sexually integrated, you need to live from your sexual centre, so that turn-on and desire are no longer relegated to the bedroom, and you live a life of feeling. We've all done the non-feeling thing, and it didn't work. We're not automatons. Our feelings are an imperative component of our experience as humans. So, to be sexually integrated, you need to be able to access the full feeling scope – the good, the icky, the epic – all of it.

Glossary of terms

Anal (sex): intercourse with a bum hole

Animalistic: being free and embodying a quality of wildness

Backing off: dialling back the speed and intensity of sex to extend the experience

Big dick energy: embodied and powerful manhood, no matter the size of one's penis

Blow your load: ejaculation. Can be used for male or female ejaculators.

Bobble head: a person with an over-inflated mind who spends their time thinking instead of feeling

Bodacious: a very attractive body

Boning: having sexual intercourse

Bonking: having sexual intercourse

Boy-man celeb: a famous man who is yet to integrate the true essence of his masculinity and often acts like a boy. Sometimes in public.

Carnal: primal desires and needs

Cock: a penis

Cock gazing: when a man looks at his own penis with the intention to heal and re-discover his body and sexuality

Corporeal: of the human body

Cum: to ejaculate

Cummy: feeling like one might orgasm sometime soon.

Cunt: a vulva

Dick: a penis

Dry hump: rubbing on another in a sexual way while wearing clothes

Eruption: when lava spews out of a volcano, except the lava is sperm and the volcano is a penis

Fanny: a vulva

Femininity: the pure and potent essence of a feminine being, usually a woman

Flaccid: soft penis

Flesh suit: the human body

Flogging the dolphin: masturbating for men (the dolphin being the penis)

Frou frou: a vulva (and an early noughties band)

Get down: hip slang for coitus

Get off: to orgasm

Heart-centred: to feel and act through love

Heavy petting: rubbing strongly

Hit it and quit it: go get in, do the job at hand and leave soon after (usually as it pertains to fucking someone)

Hot spots: erogenous zones i.e., genitals, nipples, arm pits, etc.

Jack hammer: having strong and repetitive penetrative sex like the machine used for digging up roads

Jack rabbiting: having fast sex like a furry bunny

Jerking off: masturbating a penis

Johnson: penis

Leader boy: similar to boy-man celeb but in positions of leadership and not celebrity

Lettuce hands lover: someone who touches with tentative hands that are non-committal and are afraid to offend

Mandurance: the energy of cultivated sexual stamina for men

Masculinity: the pure and potent essence of a masculine being, usually a man

Minge: a hairy pussy (but not super-hairy)

Muff: a substantial puff of hair on a pussy

Noggin: a head

Normie: a 'normal' person who isn't very conscious

Peach: a juicy vulva

Pelvic-thrust sex: sex that engages only the hips

Poon: a vulva.

Possibility mindset: a state of mind that is solution focussed, not problem focused

Power language: words voiced with intention, depth and meaning

Primal: vital and powerful. An animalistic and raw energy.

Primal desire: a raw and wild feeling of longing

Pussy: an empowering synonym for vulva and the entire sexual centre

Pussy Gazing: when a woman looks at her own vulva with the intention to heal and re-discover her body and sexuality

Raunchy: dirty and nasty, of sexual connotation

Re-wilded: returning to wildness, specifically after being tamed or domesticated

Riding cowgirl: a sexual position where a woman is sitting on the lap of her partner

Ritual(istic): making something sacred and intentional

Rub one out: to masturbate

Rumpy pumpy: to have sexual intercourse without intention or connection to self or other

Schlong: a penis

Screw: to have sexual intercourse

Sex bomb goddess: a very powerful and sensual woman who is connected to her sexuality

Sexual pizazz: being exciting or attractive in an erotic way

Sexy serpents: snake-like creatures that are moving and connecting in an erotic fashion

Shaft-stroke: to rub the body of the penis with the intention of generating pleasure for the man

Shag: to have sexual intercourse

Shagging: people in the act of sexual intercourse

Shaking hands with Mr Winky: to masturbate a penis

Shame hangover: when someone has shared vulnerably and later feels unsure about what they've said

Skank it: to get down and sexy

Soul-attunement: to be in balance and alignment with the essence of one's life-force

Spank the monkey: to masturbate a penis

Swirling: circular manual motions to illicit pleasure

Tapping: rhythmic petting or finger slaps, generally done on anuses or pussies

Testes: the ball-bags that house the family jewels of a man

Thrusting machine: one dimensional penetrative sex that mimics what a rudimentary sex machine would do

Tit for tat: when someone does something that seems untoward and the other does a similar act in return to level the playing field

Tugging: stretching and pulling the penis (or nipple, ear-lobe – you choose), to create pleasure

Wank: to masturbate

Wanky: uncool, pretentious, silly

Wholeness: being and living from a place of pure expression of all parts of the self

Willy: a penis

Acknowledgements

Thank you to our students, clients, podcast listeners and community for showing up for this work and being so open to receiving our insights, stories and teachings. Your resonance with our journey is the number one reason this work has come so far.

Thank you to our parents – Gloria and Phil, Lynne and Paul, and Ross and Kathryn – and our families for their ongoing support, no matter what we do (including having sex on a podcast).

Thank you to our agent, Adam Gauntlett of PFD, for asking us if we'd write this book and suggesting this title, which we originally cringed at and now adore. To our editor, Jillian Young, for being such a champion of our work and for helping us with ease, grace and adeptness to take our initial manuscript and scrub it up into the book you're now holding in your hands. To the whole team at Piatkus, including Jillian Stewart, Bekki Guyatt and Matthew Crossey, thank you for helping to shape this book and bring it into the world.

All our love and gratitude to our dear friends, including but not limited to Beam, Claire, Aurora, Joseph, Katya, Andy, David and Rohan, who encouraged and supported us at every stage of this project.

And thanks to you, dear reader, for choosing to come together.